PLAYING
WITH
PURPOSE

PLAYING
WITH
PURPOSE

Inside the Lives and Faith of
the NFL's Top New Quarterbacks—
Sam Bradford, Colt McCoy, and Tim Tebow

MIKE YORKEY

BARBOUR
PUBLISHING

Cover images: Sam Bradford: AP Photo/Charlie Riedel
          Tim Tebow: © Erik S. Lesser/Reuters/Corbis
          Colt McCoy: AP Photo/Matt Slocum

The author is represented by WordServe Literary Group, Ltd., Greg Johnson, Literary Agent, 10152 S. Knoll Circle, Highlands Ranch, CO 80130

Published by Barbour Publishing, Inc., P.O. Box 719, Uhrichsville, Ohio 44683
www.barbourbooks.com

Our mission is to publish and distribute inspirational products offering exceptional value and biblical encouragement to the masses.

ecpa Member of the
Evangelical Christian
Publishers Association

Printed in the United States of America.

CONTENTS

INTRODUCTION

Fellow football fans, we're in for a treat.

With the kickoff of the National Football League's 2010 season, we get to sit back in our Stratoloungers and watch three rookie quarterbacks—Sam Bradford, Colt McCoy, and Tim Tebow—make their mark in America's most popular sport. Armed with DirecTV's NFL Sunday Ticket and holding remotes in our hands, we'll have front row seats for all the action.

It promises to be quite a show.

Sam Bradford, Colt McCoy, and Tim Tebow—listed here in alphabetical order—are three special young men who performed spectacularly for the universities of Oklahoma, Texas, and Florida, respectively. They've been groomed for greatness since high school, and they burst into our living rooms as college freshmen (though only Tim played as a true freshman) when they were handed the responsibility of guiding high-powered NCAA football programs down the field.

Instead of collapsing under the weight of the high expectations placed on their shoulder pads, though, they became folk heroes to their fans and focal points of television and radio coverage on ESPN, CBS, Fox Sports, and regional football networks. They passed, they scored . . . they praised the Lord.

During their storied collegiate careers, the Three QBs led their teams to Bowl Championship Series (BCS) National Championship games, set numerous passing records, bounced back from injuries, fought for the Heisman Trophy, and generated tons of heat on hundreds, if not thousands, of Internet "fan blogs."

The raves, rumors, rants, and outright falsehoods posted in cyberspace weren't a phenomenon just 10 or 15 years ago, but they're the reality of playing today at the most visible and talked-about position in football on three of the most successful and high-profile college teams in the country. As Sam, Colt, and Tim would tell you, they get too much credit when their teams win and too much blame when their teams lose. But they'd also tell you it comes with the territory.

Now these larger-than-life QBs are stepping onto the national stage of professional football, and it's a matter of *when*—not *if*—they will get their chance to call plays in an NFL huddle. Once they're handed the reins, you'll see the media machine rev up to hyper levels. The football pundits will trip over themselves to offer opinions on whether Sam Bradford can turn around the St. Louis Rams franchise, whether Colt McCoy can take the Cleveland Browns back to the playoffs, or whether Tim Tebow can show the football world he can play quarterback in the NFL with the Denver Broncos.

These are called "story lines" in the TV production trucks, which is why the Three QBs promise to be the subject of scrutiny, the topic of sports talk shows, and the recipients of hosannas as well as Bronx cheers in coming years. They certainly won't be ignored. If their football careers continue on the same arc, Sam, Colt, or Tim will become a household name in *every* part of the country, not just the football hotbeds of Oklahoma, Texas, and Florida.

So who are Sam Bradford, Colt McCoy, and Tim Tebow? What makes this triumvirate of quarterback talent so compelling?

You'll find the answers in *Playing with Purpose: Inside the Lives and Faith of the NFL's Top New Quarterbacks*. The following pages will

- introduce Sam, Colt, and Tim and describe where they came from and how they grew up;
- tell you about how their parents raised them and what their families are like;
- narrate their start in football, including their junior high and high school years;
- recap their stellar collegiate careers;
- chronicle their tough moments;
- discuss the implications of the 2010 NFL draft;
- show their willingness to use their incredible, one-in-a-million platforms to talk about their personal relationship with the Lord of the Universe—Jesus Christ.

All three of these young football players were raised in Christian homes, so none of them has a "hell-raising testimony" to share—thank goodness. But they would tell you they've had their share of ups and downs in life, just like anyone else.

Keep in mind that these three young men have been leading public lives since their senior years in high school. Today,
they are caught up in a media vortex where they can't order
a second dessert without having this breathtaking news reported on the ESPN crawl.

In a sense, they've grown up before our eyes, and by any
measuring stick, they've done themselves and their families
proud by the way they've handled themselves following tremendous victories and bone-crushing defeats in some of college football's biggest games played before packed stadiums
and national television viewers numbering in the tens of millions.

Yet it's also worth noting how these three young quarterbacks have acted when no one was looking. A small-but-tell-
ing example of character: two-thirds of the 96 Florida Gators
football players who played or were on scholarship in 2009
had received traffic citations since 2006 in Alachua County,
home to the Gainesville campus of the University of Florida.
The number of traffic citations issued to those players: 251.
The number of traffic citations issued to Tim Tebow during
his four-year college football career: zero. "Though authori-
ties reportedly look the other way when he jaywalks on
water," quipped Dwight Perry of *The Seattle Times*.

Tim Tebow hasn't walked on water, and neither has Sam
Bradford or Colt McCoy, but that hasn't stopped them from
talking about the Person who *has*—Jesus Christ. The biggest thing that sets the Three QBs apart from their peers is
their boldness in sharing their faith in Christ. They did that
through high school and college, and they don't appear to be
audibilizing—changing the play at the line of scrimmage—as

they enter the pro ranks. Apparently, they learned the invaluable lesson that if you make a stand early on, you only have to make it once.

As any youth pastor will tell you, telling the world you're a Christian—knowing that you'll be mocked and made fun of—takes more guts than completing a fourth-and-goal pass into the end zone when your team is down by four points with five seconds left. But wearing their faith on the sleeves of their football jerseys—or inscribing Bible verses on their eye black, à la Tim Tebow—is part of what makes these three quarterbacks so special.

"I've interviewed all three players, and I can't differentiate them," said Jill Ewert, editor of *Sharing the Victory* magazine, which is published by the Fellowship of Christian Athletes (FCA). "I can't put Tim on a pedestal any higher than Sam or Colt because all three of these guys just knocked my socks off. What's pleased me has been watching them succeed and how God has allowed them to fail in graceful ways."

Reagan Lambert, FCA director at the University of Texas campus, said he's never seen three young men like Sam, Colt, and Tim come along at the same time. "People have used the term 'perfect storm' for a lot of different things," he said, "and I believe that's what we've witnessed with three strong Christian young men, who all played the quarterback position, leading major college programs to national titles and winning Heisman Trophies. I don't think we'll ever see anything like it again."

WHY A BOOK LIKE
PLAYING WITH PURPOSE?

Like the convergence of three funnel clouds in Tornado Alley, Sam Bradford, Colt McCoy, and Tim Tebow *are* the perfect storm of quarterbacking talent. Their on- and off-the-field exploits have inspired millions of words to be written about them, and they've been the subjects of hundreds of magazine articles and TV features. They have surely lost count of the number of times they've been interviewed. While they shared large chunks of their life stories during their college years, we will have to wait until they decide to write their autobiographies for a full accounting.

When—and, again, not *if*—any of the three has a breakout season, we can be sure we'll see Sam's, Colt's, or Tim's autobiography hit the bookshelves. This is why their agents have undoubtedly instructed them not to cooperate with any book projects, including this one. But since these three have talked extensively with the media ever since their days as high school pups—and people close to them have been interviewed for *Playing with Purpose*—you can enjoy this fascinating book in the meantime.

GAME DAY

Chances are strong that you know football is the most popular and most watched sport on television in America today. "Game Day" can only mean one thing: there's a big football game to be played—and in today's hyped-up sports culture, *every* football game seems to qualify as being of great importance, momentous, pivotal, crucial, or even historic. If a buck were thrown into the pot every time a football analyst said, "This is a big game for both teams," we could retire the national debt in no time.

In the buildup for the "big game," the spotlight always falls on the quarterback, the most important player on the field. He is the team leader, the player the other 10 members of the offense expect to "move the chains" and lead them into the end zone.

Every play begins with the quarterback crouched underneath the center or positioned five to seven yards behind the line of scrimmage in the "shotgun" formation. His eyes scan the defensive side of the football, and in just a couple of seconds, he must locate where the defensive players are positioned and deduce what the defense will do to stop him and his teammates. He has the ability to change course at the line of scrimmage if he believes the defense is lined up perfectly to stop the play that the offensive coordinator or head coach has called.

Once he barks out signals to his offense and yells "hut" to start the play, the ball is literally in the quarterback's hands. He can hand off the pigskin to a running back, lateral to a teammate, drop back and pass the ball downfield, or run the ball himself. His ability to make split-second decisions, fend off ferocious pass rushes, hit his receivers with precision passes, and take a late hit separates the skill set of a quarterback from those of other players. Because the permutations are countless, and because of their ability to inspire their teammates, execute plays, read defenses, and throw the ball *exactly* where it needs to be, quarterbacks are the most dissected, most discussed, most well-known, and most controversial players on the team.

As the quarterback goes, so goes the team—and that is why football pundits devote so much time to "breaking down" the strengths and weakness of the opposing quarterbacks during a pregame buildup. Quarterbacks shoulder the responsibility of whether the team wins or loses, and that role is not for the faint of heart. Simply said, quarterback is the hardest, riskiest, toughest, and greatest position in all of sports.

Quarterbacks live under a microscope. The scrutiny never lets up. Fans drive by their homes at all hours of the day, and when they eat at a restaurant, they are constantly interrupted for autographs and pictures. They know that fans form lifelong opinions based upon chance encounters, so they always have to be on their guard. They understand that fans will never tell 20 people that their QB was courteous and nice, but they will tell 20 people that he blew them off.

This is the Faustian bargain that top-flight quarterbacks must accept—the fishbowl existence and the anonymous criticism. Yet, as Green Bay Packers quarterback Aaron Rodgers says, "Anytime I'm recognized and can't just walk around, I remind myself that I haven't had a [real] job in my life."

Do know that quarterbacks work hard—insanely hard. They put incredible numbers of hours into becoming the go-to guy on the gridiron. Even though Colt, at 24 years of age, is the oldest of the Three QBs at the start of the 2010 NFL season (Tim is 23, and Sam is just 22), all three have been doing this quarterback thing for a long time—more than half their lives. They all started playing organized football in elementary school and set their sights on becoming the starting quarterbacks for their high school teams. (Tim's case is a bit different, as you'll discover; he chose his high school because he didn't attend one. If that sounds confusing, it's because he was homeschooled until he enrolled at the University of Florida.)

From the time their voices started to change during puberty through the preparations for their "pro days" in the spring of 2010, Sam, Colt, and Tim have been throwing down-and-outs and post patterns to their receivers for hours on end. They've learned hundreds of plays and dozens of formations—and practiced them until they became second nature. They've spent their evenings watching game film until their eyeballs hurt. And if they didn't get it right, their coaches chewed them out.

Practice, practice, practice. What football fans see when the curtain is raised on Friday nights, Saturday afternoons, and Sunday afternoons is far different from what they would see during the countless hours of preparation—the pianist's equivalent of practicing hand position, scales, arpeggios, and complete pieces—that take place on the practice field five or six days a week for five to six months a year.

Yet for all the practicing under their coaches' watchful eyes, all three quarterbacks had Achilles' heels leading up to the NFL draft—all of which involved their shoulders and throwing arms.

Sam injured his throwing shoulder in the 2009 season opener against Brigham Young, causing him to miss the next three games. When he returned, he reinjured his shoulder against Texas and then submitted to season-ending surgery for the reconstruction of his acromioclavicular (AC) joint.

After giving himself time to heal, Sam began the rehabilitation process to strengthen his shoulder so he could impress

NFL scouts in the spring of 2010, prior to the draft. At his pro day on March 29, before representatives from 21 NFL teams, Sam hit just about every note, completing 49 of 50 passes with pinpoint precision, tight spirals, and excellent velocity.

Colt McCoy suffered his shoulder injury on college football's biggest stage—the BCS Championship game between Texas and Alabama, which was played at the Rose Bowl on January 7, 2010. On the Longhorns' fifth play from scrimmage, Colt was scrambling to his right when he was hammered by Alabama's defensive lineman Marcel Dareus, who scrunched Colt's right shoulder into the Rose Bowl's grass turf. Colt didn't return to action, and that severely lessened the 'Horns' chances of winning (Texas eventually caved in to the Crimson Tide, losing 37–21). But at his pro day, Colt put on a passing clinic, completing all 55 passes in a controlled workout.

Tim Tebow didn't have a shoulder injury to overcome, but he spent three months earlier in 2010 reworking his throwing mechanics. CBS television analyst and former Baltimore Ravens coach Brian Billick roundly criticized Tim during his final college game—the 2010 Sugar Bowl—for carrying the ball too low as he dropped back to pass, which resulted in a loopy throwing motion and long windup delivery.

After working with a series of high-profile experts, including former NFL coaches Sam Wyche and Jon Gruden, to eliminate the swooping windup, Tim changed his throwing motion—as well as the conventional wisdom that he was second- or third-round draft material, a "project" destined for an apprenticeship role in the NFL. Tim shook the football world and became easily the biggest surprise of the 2010 NFL draft when the Denver Broncos made him a first-round pick and 25th overall.

Those are just a few of the story lines that will be hashed out during the 2010 NFL season and beyond. Although the game of football itself is as unpredictable as how the ball bounces off the turf, one thing seems certain: Sam Bradford, Colt McCoy, and Tim Tebow are bona fide football heroes worthy of our interest. They come along at a time when too many football stars disappoint their fans with news reports of the latest paternity suit or run-in at the local strip club.

Yes, Sam, Colt, and Tim are human—regular guys who grew up in intact families—and they would want us to know that. But it will be interesting to follow their ascent as they take their quarterbacking skills to the "next level"—the NFL—and face the slings and arrows of the media and the blogosphere.

While Tim Tebow was living in an off-campus apartment as a student at the University of Florida, he kept a framed poem on his wall that included the words, "Little eyes are watching you." That saying, no doubt, was a reminder to Tim that children looked up to him—a college-age quarterback playing every year for a national championship.

Now that Tim, Sam, and Colt have graduated to the NFL, they have become multimillionaires—and with all the riches and fame associated with playing professional football, the world is their oyster.

But thanks to their core values and their strength of character—which we can credit in large part to the way their Christian parents raised them—the feeling here is that none of the Three QBs will forget that little eyes are still watching them.

1

SAM BRADFORD:
THE DYNAMITE DRAFT PICK

He's got that tall, lanky build and that tight, curly hair that reminds you of Napoleon Dynamite, the listless, underachieving star of the cult classic film by the same name.

But that's where the similarity ends.

Sam Bradford, the University of Oklahoma quarterback the past three seasons, could probably throw a football over the mountains, as Napoleon's Uncle Rico bragged he could do in the movie. But Sam's long, long bomb would hit the receiver in mid-stride.

Napoleon would call that "flippin' sweet."

Sam had the shortest college career of the Three QBs, playing one year less and losing most of the 2009 season to injury. Despite appearing in the fewest games and receiving less national attention than Colt or Tim, he could be the best quarterback of the three. At least that's what the St. Louis Rams were betting when they voted with their checkbook and tabbed Sam as the No. 1 pick in the 2010 NFL draft.

As they say in draft-speak, Sam brings tons of "upside" to the table: excellent height, superior arm, pinpoint accuracy, and rock-solid pocket awareness. He is the tallest of the Three QBs, standing 6 feet, 4¼ inches—the fourth of an inch must be important because it's usually included whenever Sam's height is listed. Since the end of 2009, he's added 13 pounds of muscle to his frame. Scouts believe the extra bulk will make him more durable in the NFL and that it may even bolster his rocket arm.

The scouting reports also say that Sam is an "elite decision-maker." He processes information quickly and can work through the "progressions" of the play, meaning he can look for receivers in a certain order and then complete the pass to his second or third target if his primary receiver isn't open. When his golden arm unleashes the ball, the pass whizzes through the air like it's attached to a zip line—a frozen rope, the scouts call it.

But Sam didn't always have a monster arm, and of the Three QBs, he's the latest bloomer of the bunch. In fact, he needed a huge break just to get his shot at playing quarterback for the University of Oklahoma.

THE EARLY YEARS
Samuel Jacob Bradford was born November 8, 1987, making him the youngest of the Three QBs by three months—and the only one without siblings. Since Kent and Martha Bradford were married eight years before Sam arrived, one could conjecture that she either had a hard time getting pregnant or couldn't have more children. Whatever the reason, they

slathered Sam with love and devotion. He was their pride and joy, and his athletic career would benefit from the extra attention they were able to afford him.

WHERE'S RUDY WHEN YOU NEED HIM?

The mid-1970s were glory years for Oklahoma football. When Kent Bradford was a student, back in those pre-BCS days, the Barry Switzer-coached teams captured four Big Eight titles and one national championship.

Before Kent played his junior and senior years for the Sooners, however, he was on the scout team—the scrubs and underclassmen who weren't good enough, or who weren't ready, to suit up on Saturday afternoons. Think Rudy at Notre Dame.

One afternoon during practice, the scout team coach, Steve Barrett, instructed Kent—an offensive tackle—to block starting defensive lineman Lee Roy Selmon.

That was a tall order. At 6 feet, 3 inches tall and weighing 256 pounds, "The Gentle Giant" would go on to become the No. 1 pick in the 1976 NFL draft and fashion a Hall of Fame career playing for the Tampa Bay Buccaneers. The guy was a load.

The play was run, and Lee Roy blew past Kent like he was a cardboard cutout. When the offense retreated to the huddle, Coach Barrett yelled, "Bradford, can't you block that guy?"

"Coach, if I would block him, I'd be starting. I wouldn't be on this scout team," Kent answered. "Besides, you probably don't have anybody who'd have blocked him, either."

Now there's a football player who knows what's happening on the field.

Sam, who was born in Oklahoma City, Oklahoma, got his size from his father, who played as an offensive lineman at the University of Oklahoma for two seasons in 1977–78, during the Barry Switzer era. But don't get the idea that just because Dad was a proud OU alum, baby Sam was dressed in red jumpers with OU insignias. His mom graduated from the intrastate rival Oklahoma State University (where Kent's father, Bill, happened to play football in the 1940s), so they had what those in Oklahoma circles might call a "mixed marriage."

One time, before baby Sam turned a year old, Mom took him to a portrait studio where the photographer had several props, including a pint-sized outfit in orange and black—Oklahoma State's school colors.

Kent arrived late to the shoot and was aghast to find his son—*his son!*—sporting an Oklahoma State outfit. When he pressed Martha for an explanation, she replied that she thought their baby son looked darling in the black-and-orange ensemble.

These days you won't find Sam digging through the photo albums and reminiscing over that incriminating photo. "I don't really like the picture," he said.

Why is that?

"Because of the attire. Wrong colors. It wasn't even Halloween."

There isn't much evidence that Martha tried to dress her son in OSU school colors after that episode. Since the University of Oklahoma is in Norman, 20 miles south of Oklahoma City—and because Kent bled Sooner red—Martha became neutral in what you could call a "Switzer-land" home. Since Kent had been an OU season ticket holder for what seemed like forever, young Sam grew up cheering for Big Red at Oklahoma Memorial Stadium. Even Mom came around during the "Bedlam" games—the annual showdown between OU and OSU—and rooted for the Sooners.

You could say sports were important in the Bradford household. Martha was an elementary school physical education teacher while Kent, who worked as an insurance agent, was the former Sooner lineman with a competitive nature. When Sam was a preschooler, they filled his bedroom with different kinds of balls, bats, and gloves. Nothing like getting him started early.

Sam's aunt, Jan Bradford, remembers coming over to the house and having Sam, then a preschooler, lead her to his room so he could show off his ball collection—one ball at a time.

"Here's a football!"

"Here's a baseball!"

"Here's a golf ball!"

The only thing Sam didn't bring out during this show-and-tell was his ice skates. His love affair with the ice started because Kent and Martha enjoyed ice skating at a nearby rink during the winter months. When Sam was five years old, he asked for his own pair of skates for Christmas. He wanted to play hockey because it looked like a fun sport.

Santa did his part, making sure the ice skates were under the tree. The parents did their part by immediately enrolling Sam in skating lessons. But the kindergartner didn't like it when the coach got tough on him. One day, the tearful youngster came home and announced he wanted to quit skating.

Mom hugged her son but remained firm. The family had paid for 12 lessons, so he had to see this through. If he stuck with it, then he could play hockey.

Sam completed his skating lessons, and when he began his elementary school years, he starting playing hockey—but he also liked the Big Three All-American sports: football, basketball, and baseball.

Sam displayed some of his athletic precociousness on the ball field as a nine-year-old when he played for the Putnam City Optimist Ducks, who won the AAU state baseball championship in 1997. Check this out: the Ducks played more than 65 games that year, and their state championship team of third and fourth graders earned a trip to Sherwood, Arkansas, for the national tournament.

NO SOCCER FOR SAM

By the 1990s, youth soccer—played under the auspices of the American Youth Soccer Organization (AYSO)—was taking up every free field between Portland, Maine, and Portland, Oregon. In many households, "bunch ball" was replacing T-ball as the sport of choice.

Sam Bradford played just about every sport under the sun—or on the ice—growing up, but he never played organized soccer. Sure, he outplayed the kids in his class during elementary school recess, but his parents never signed him up to play soccer, most likely because they were running themselves ragged getting Sam to all his football, basketball, baseball, and hockey games.

"I would say if you put me on a soccer field today, I would be clueless," Sam said.

No, Sam, you'd probably figure out the game pretty quickly.

No sooner had Sam thrown his mitt into his bedroom closet at the end of summer than it was time to slip on the shoulder pads and a helmet for youth football. Sam somehow always seemed to play each fall on teams named the "Sooners"—with their fire engine red mesh jerseys. Then, by Thanksgiving time, the chilly climate made it easy for Sam to transition into basketball, which was played indoors in gymnasiums. After basketball season was over, the sports merry-go-round started all over again with spring baseball.

And then there was hockey.

CATCHING THE HOCKEY BUG

In those early years, Sam's father would drop by his son's bedroom to tuck him in. Many evenings, he would ask his son to say 10 things to him—positive statements like "I can do anything I think I can." Kent was planting the seed that young Sam could do anything he set his mind to, but realizing his goals meant he would have to work hard. Nothing would be handed to him—on the field or in the classroom. It was up to him to set a goal and go chase after it.

That's one way to build a champion, but if you were to ask Sam what his favorite sport was back in grade school and middle school, he'd tell you it wasn't football, basketball, or baseball. That's because he had caught the hockey bug.

Sam was a multi-sport kid juggling a year-round schedule of games "in season," but he truly loved hockey and displayed a gift for the game. His idol was National Hockey League star Pavel Bure—the "Russian Rocket" who played for the Vancouver Canucks and led the NHL in goals during the 1993–94 season.

Despite the time commitment required to keep his hand in the other three sports, it wasn't long before Sam won a spot on the Oklahoma City Junior Blazers, a competitive "travel team" that either drove or flew to tournaments as far away as St. Louis, Kansas City, Dallas, and Houston.

We're talking serious junior hockey. Canadian-born Mike McEwen, a talented defenseman who helped the New York Islanders win three Stanley Cups in the early 1980s, coached the team.

As Sam developed his love for ice hockey in his middle school years, he adopted the Canucks as his favorite team. He would wake up early and grab the morning newspaper so he could see if Vancouver won and if his hero Pavel Bure scored a goal—or two or three.

Then one day, Sam asked his parents—in all seriousness—if the family could move to Vancouver, Canada, the home of the Canucks, so he could watch Pavel roam the ice in person. And besides, they played the best junior hockey in Canada, eh?

"I told him, 'We can't move to Canada. Our lives are in Oklahoma,' " his father said in *USA Hockey* magazine. "But he was pretty set on it."

Sam's parents' practical thinking prevailed, and the family stayed put in Oklahoma City.

Playing on a hockey travel team was a good news/bad news situation for Sam and his parents—and quite a commitment. The good news was that Sam played a top-flight schedule against the best teams in the Midwest. The bad news was the constant travel, which meant being away from home a couple of weekends a month and competing in tournaments where games could be scheduled for six or seven o'clock in the morning or after nine at night. (Tournament games had to be played morning, noon, and night because of the scarcity of rink time.) Sam's parents said he never griped about the early face-offs, though there were 5 a.m. wake-up calls when they had to stuff Sam's legs into his hockey pants while he was still asleep.

From every indication, though, the family enjoyed their hockey days with Sam. Kent never complained about being a "hockey dad," and Martha never complained about being a "hockey mom." Consequently, Sam didn't grow up a complainer, either.

"I definitely think their attitudes had a great deal of impact on getting me where I am today," Sam told *The Oklahoman.*

Sam played two years on the OC Junior Blazers, and his leadership qualities and ever-improving stick skills landed him the role of team captain. But as high school loomed, decisions had to be made. The start of high school is the time when most athletes have to "specialize" in their best—or favorite—sport. Was Sam going to become a hockey player and chuck football, basketball, and baseball?

Mike McEwen told Kent his kid could one day play in the National Hockey League. Sam was a natural, the coach said. He had good hands, great vision, and played smart on the ice.

Kent listened to the old NHL hockey player make his case, saying nothing as his patronizing smile grew bigger and bigger. The father wouldn't be persuaded. Kent had other things in mind for his son, and they weren't going to happen on a sheet of ice.

MEET SAM BRADFORD, CELLO PLAYER

When he was in fourth grade, Sam started playing the cello, a lower-sounding member of the string family that is held between the knees and played in the seated position. He kept at it through middle school, when he became part of the orchestra at Cooper Middle School.

As is often the case with grade-school musicians, Sam's cello ended up in a closet when he graduated to Putnam City North High School. Too much homework and too many sports: football in the fall, basketball in winter, and baseball or golf in the spring.

Sam's father told the *New York Times* that he played the cello "okay for his age group"—although his football coaches at Putnam North and the University of Oklahoma gushed about the quarterback who played the cello. Some of the media's "cello-playing quarterback" storyline was embellished a tad, especially when the writer sought to do a little myth-building.

But Sam Bradford, quarterback/cello player, has a nice ring to it, doesn't it?

THE TRANSITION YEARS

In the 1960s and 1970s, when Kent and Martha were growing up, youth sports weren't nearly as organized as they later became. Youth league presidents risked the wrath of parents if they scheduled baseball, basketball, football, or hockey games on Sunday mornings. That was the time for church. For worshipping God.

That mindset slowly changed in the 1980s as parents sought better and better competition for their children, and by the time Sam was lacing up his cleats, sneakers, or hockey skates in the mid-1990s, all the barriers came crashing down. The advent of "all-star" leagues and travel teams heralded a new era in youth sports, and the Bradfords plugged right into the program. Sam was always playing a sport—against the best competition in his peer group—and Kent and Martha had their share of Sunday morning games to attend. Since the seasons overlapped, they had to make choices about which games Sam would play in. That was the reality they had carved for themselves.

By the time Sam entered fifth grade, Martha noticed something else: even though their son was gaining valuable athletic experience every weekend, he was missing out on something far more important—learning about God. She knew that instilling spiritual values and good morals in Sam would mean a lot more than him learning the fast break, the two-minute offense, or the power play. Mom believed it was time for the family to start going to church. If a game was scheduled for a Sunday morning, the team would have to play without Sam.

"We were playing sports every weekend, and it's not like I didn't know who God was, but it was just something that we really did not have the time to do," Sam told Jenni Carlson, a sports columnist with *The Oklahoman*. "I think my mom finally brought it up and was like, 'Hey, we're going to start going to church.' We started going to a couple of different churches, and finally, we found one where a couple of my friends attended. I give a lot of credit to my friends; they were the ones who got me involved in youth group, got me involved in Confirmation, got me to really stick with it."

When Sam started attending church regularly, he sat with

his parents in "big church"—the main congregation—and probably had his share of those fidgety moments any fifth or sixth grader would have. Then his friends asked him if he wanted to join them in the middle school ministry. That's when church became fun and interesting to the youngster.

Hanging out with friends, listening to an engaging middle school pastor, and hearing the gospel was a great package, and it was in seventh grade that Sam made a decision that would affect the direction of the rest of his life. "I remember going every Sunday morning, just listening and learning more about the Lord," he said in an interview with Shawn Brown on the CBN network. "Probably after a couple of months, I really decided that I wanted to give my life to the Lord. And ever since then, it's something that I really try to make a strong point in my life."

Sam was also getting stronger as an athlete as he entered Putnam City North, a four-year public high school of 2,000 students situated in the Bradfords' upper-class neighborhood in Oklahoma City. Putnam City North High was one of three high schools in their district: Putnam City and Putnam City West were the other two. The three Putnam City high schools, which were among the largest in the state, competed in the highest classification in Oklahoma: 6A.

Academically, Putnam North was among the highest-scoring public schools in Oklahoma. Before Sam came along, Putnam North's most famous alumni was James Marsden (class of '91), an actor who played the superhero Cyclops in the three X-Men films and also appeared in other Hollywood features like *Superman Returns*, *Hairspray*, and *Enchanted*.

Something had to be cut from Sam's top-heavy sports

schedule, and the family decided it would have to be ice hockey. That was because of the time-consuming travel and weird practice times associated with hockey, plus the fact that, well, Sam couldn't play the other sports that he was really, *really* good at—like football and basketball.

MAKING A CHOICE

There was another issue to deal with as Sam entered high school: he was growing like prairie tallgrass. His growth spurt started in eighth grade, and his knees were killing him as he ran up and down the basketball floor in a summer league before his freshman year. Sam was growing so fast that Mom couldn't keep him in clothes, especially jeans.

Sam hit 6 feet, 3 inches during his first year of high school, an inch—and a quarter!—under his present height. He was rail thin, as most high school freshman are. When Sam tried out for quarterback of the ninth-grade football team, he wowed his coaches and teammates. Varsity coach Bob Wilson, who likes to know if he has any good-looking signal-callers in the pipeline, kept his eye on the spindly kid.

Then it was on to basketball season and another freshman team. In seventh and eighth grades, basketball was probably the sport Sam played most. He spent his summers with an AAU traveling team that moved around like the Harlem Globetrotters: tournaments were played in Indiana, Georgia, Virginia, Missouri, Kansas, Colorado, and even Las Vegas. As Sam displayed his talents as a great shooter and rebounder during the first month of the season, the Putnam North coaches bumped him up to the varsity team—as a freshman.

Since Sam didn't get much playing time with the juniors

and seniors on the varsity basketball team, he still played in the freshman games—which were scheduled for different days of the week (Monday and Thursday) than the varsity games (Tuesday and Friday).

NO OFFSEASON

There was no such thing as "downtime" for Sam during his childhood. So was he worried about burnout?

"I'm glad there was never a break," he told Andrew Gilman of *The Oklahoman*. "If I had to think about those season-ending losses for seven months, that would be terrible. This way, I just go right into another sport."

For Kent and Martha Bradford, sitting in the bleachers for four basketball games a week was a piece of cake. They'd been doing that sort of stuff since Sam was in short pants. Then springtime blossomed, the time of year when young boys' hearts turn toward . . . golf.

Golf? What about baseball? Wasn't Sam a flame-throwing pitcher and a big bat at the plate?

Sure, but Sam found golf a welcome change from team sports. The competition was between him and the golf course, not other players, and he got to play with his friends. So yes, Sam was a golfer, too—and golf was *another* sport he excelled at.

That's one of *five* if you're keeping score at home.

By now, you're probably wondering, *When did Sam have time to play golf?* Who knows? But Sam started playing when he was 10 years old and proved himself quite a natural from tee to green.

One time, on a hot summer day when Sam was still in elementary school, Martha Bradford dropped him and a couple buddies off at a local par-3 course—a nine-holer. A golf marathon was planned for that day, and Sam and his buddies made more than 12 circuits of the municipal track before darkness fell. Total number of holes played: 110.

Sam remembers sleeping well that night.

Then there was the time he got the first of his *four* holes in one. He was just a kid playing a round with his grandfather at the time. They came up to a par-3, where Sam had clanged the ball off the flagstick the day before.

Sam looked at his grandpa. "I hit the pin yesterday," he said. "I'm going to make it today."

His grandfather gave him an encouraging *Be my guest* wave, then watched the boy fashion a swing. The ball rose in flight, landed on the green, and plunked into the cup. In other words, Sam jarred it for a hole in one.

Although the odds of making a hole in one are astronomical—one in 12,750, according to *Golf Digest* magazine—Sam made it look easy. Golf was just another sport where he outshined the competition. By the time he was in high school, Sam regularly shot in the 70s and would become a scratch golfer—someone who could break par for a round of golf.

THE SOPHOMORE WINS THE JOB

Putnam North football coach Bob Wilson was in his early fifties when Sam Bradford arrived in the summer of 2003 for the start of a new season. This was his eleventh year of coaching the Panther football team and his seventeenth high school season overall, so he knew something about coaching boys—including the canyon-wide gap in maturity between sophomores and seniors. That's why his teams usually had a senior quarterback under center.

In his business, that was a no-brainer: 18-year-olds were more responsible and levelheaded than amped-up 15- or 16-year-olds who were learning a complex game with many moving parts. You win games and keep parents happy when seniors play. That's why when you're an underclassman, you wait to play.

Heading into the 2003 season, it was senior Philip Poulsen's turn to play quarterback. Sure, there was this Bradford kid, but all he had under his belt was one year of freshman football. He wasn't used to playing on Friday nights in front of 6,000 friends, classmates, parents, and fans at Putnam City Stadium.

But during summer practices, before the start of school, the whistle nearly dropped out of Coach Wilson's mouth when Sam ran the offense. Throw after throw . . . on the money. Good decision after good decision. And good size—he couldn't overlook that.

Coach Wilson raised some eyebrows when he tabbed Sophomore Sam as his starting quarterback, but the seasoned coach knew he was putting the better athlete on the field. "Sam came in and showed us he was the guy," Wilson said. "I don't remember a whole lot of doubt about starting him. He was a coach's dream because when you taught Sam something, you only had to say it once. He did whatever we asked him to do. He was very coachable."

As they say in the movies, this was the start of a beautiful relationship. For the next three seasons at Putnam North, the Panthers were Sam's team.

Sam was a quarterback who felt comfortable leading by example, not by being a holler-guy. "We didn't get to see Sam a lot in the summer, but he did come into the weight room at 6:30 in the morning to lift weights with the linemen. I'm telling you, linemen respect that, and linemen will block their backsides off for a guy who they feel is one of them," Wilson said.

A month into Sophomore Sam's first season as a high school varsity quarterback, he was invited to the Oklahoma State Fair for a "Midway Challenge" organized by *The Oklahoman* newspaper. With the greasy smell of Indian tacos and deep-fried Twinkies hanging in the air, Sam and three other standout quarterbacks were asked to throw a mini-football at a seven-inch star from a distance of 15 feet. Could any of these star athletes hit the tiny target and win an oversized stuffed bear at the football-toss game on the midway?

Out of 18 total throws from the four quarterbacks, there were only three hits. Guess who took home a green-and-purple dragon and a giant white teddy bear after making two strikes?

Sam Bradford, of course.

A LOVE FOR FOOTBALL

Just a month into his first season, Sam was impressing coaches and sportswriters, the latter declaring that he could be one of the best players in the state—even though he was only a sophomore. The young quarterback led the Panthers to the playoffs, where they lost in the state 6A semifinals. Sam put up some nice stats, too: 1,714 yards in passing and 11 touchdowns for the season.

MEET SAM BRADFORD, HIGH SCHOOL SOPHOMORE QUARTERBACK

Imagine you're 15 years old when an enterprising reporter at the local newspaper asks you to fill in the blanks on a list of questions. Here's how Sam answered a questionnaire from *The Oklahoman* on September 4, 2003—obviously before iPods destroyed the CD player market:

Position: quarterback

Grade: sophomore

Height, weight: 6-4, 180 pounds

Favorite movie: *2 Fast 2 Furious*

Favorite food: steak

Favorite music: rap

What's in your CD player? 50 Cent

If I were a pro wrestler, my name would be: Aztec Warrior

If I could have dinner with one person, it would be: Michael Jordan

Football was now Sam's sport. Sure, he continued playing basketball and golf at Putnam North, but his athletic future was now staked on football.

In the summer of 2004, between Sam's sophomore and junior seasons, he attended a football camp at the University of Oklahoma. The two-way street of college football camps is the kickoff of the recruiting process because it serves a dual purpose:

1. Young players improve their skills and conditioning under the watchful eyes of experienced college coaches.

2. Those same coaches take mental notes on players they'll want to recruit later on.

After squeezing the Sooners football camp into his busy schedule, Sam played well early in the 2004 season. As a team, however, the Panthers started slowly. "We were 3–3 but still had the possibility of getting to the playoffs," Coach Wilson said. "But we had to turn things around. Sam and some of the guys came up with a big sign in the locker room that said 'Believe' written on large butcher block paper. That thing crumpled during the season, but we did manage to win the next six out of the next seven games. Our comeback had a lot to do with Sam Bradford."

For someone 16 going on 17, this junior quarterback was creating quite a stir on the Putnam North campus. On the field, Sam upped his production to 1,980 yards passing and 16 touchdowns, and his quarterbacking carried the Panthers to the state playoffs. Students—and teachers—wore No. 14 jerseys to celebrate the new star in their midst. He led the Panthers to the state semifinals for the second year in a row, but the Panthers lost in the last two minutes to top-ranked Jenks, 29–23.

Sam's breakout performance in 2004 placed him squarely on the college football recruiters' radar screens. Now his name was listed on the most influential recruiting Web sites— Rivals, Scout, SuperPrep, and PrepStar College Recruiting, all of which rank players by position and identify the "blue-chippers" certain to be wooed by the major programs.

Sam wasn't at the top of anyone's pecking order, however. Some hotshot from Florida named Tim Tebow was generating a lot of buzz. Nonetheless, the recruiting derby was on. Texas Tech made the first overture in the spring of 2005 when then-head coach Mike Leach—known in the coaching fraternity for his uncanny ability to spot developing quarterbacks—offered Sam a scholarship. Sam's family also knew Texas A&M and Iowa State were sniffing around.

When Bob Wilson heard about Texas Tech's scholarship offer, the Putnam North coach picked up the phone and called his contacts inside the Oklahoma and Oklahoma State coaching staffs. *I've got a tip for you. You've got a special kid in your backyard. You better take a look at him before someone else grabs him.*

Chuck Long, then the offensive coordinator at the University of Oklahoma, didn't let much moss grow under his feet. He dropped by Putnam High in May 2005 to watch Sam throw and to meet his family. Long remembered Sam from the summer football camp, and he liked the young QB's "intangibles"—his sideline demeanor, the way he handled himself in the huddle, and his polite responsiveness to coaching. He had a cannon for an arm, but he was every bit as good in the classroom, maintaining a grade-point average of better than 4.0, which placed him in the top 10 percent of his class.

As Long and the Sooners coaching staff looked over their quarterback depth chart, they knew they had landed Rhett Bomar—the nation's No. 1 high school quarterback in the 2004 recruiting season, according to Rivals.com and Scout.com—for the coming season. Coached by his father at Grand Prairie High School in Grand Prairie, Texas, Bomar was labeled the second coming of NFL great John Elway. The Sooners' brain trust expected big things from the rangy Texan when he arrived for summer training camp.

Long and the coaching staff debated whether to toss a Sooner helmet into Sam's recruiting ring. Their thinking was that since they had Bomar, who they believed was destined for greatness, they could bring in Bradford for added depth. Perhaps the Putnam North kid would develop into a starter by his junior or senior year.

Then Long learned something about Sam that sealed the deal. "You dig a little deeper, and [you find out] he's a scratch golfer, he's a basketball player, and he's a four-sport athlete, and you like those guys, especially at the quarterback position," Long said. "But I think the scratch golf, when we found that out, [was the difference]. I learned from a professional coach that if you have a quarterback who's a scratch golfer, he's a good one because he's a strategist. He can think, he can get out of the rough, and he's thinking, 'What's the next shot?'

"Plus, it's like a four-hour match, like a football game, and there are a lot of ups and downs in that match. You have to stay even keel to get through it and play under pressure. That was really the factor that got me on board anyway, though it was a little tougher sell for the staff. But we just felt he was the guy."

Long knew that if Oklahoma waited to see how Sam performed during his senior year at Putnam City before offering him a scholarship, they would risk losing him to a rival school. The stakes were raised even higher when he heard the University of Michigan was ready to offer Sam a full ride.

This called for a preemptive strike. The Oklahoma coaching staff decided to offer Sam a scholarship at the end of his junior year so they could lock him up *before* his last season of high school football. The commitment, however, would be nonbinding since, according to NCAA rules, Sam could not officially accept an athletic scholarship until his senior season was over.

National Signing Day was always the first Wednesday in February of a high school football player's senior year. Any athlete accepting a scholarship offer before National Signing Day, like Sam did, was making an oral commitment that he could later choose to back out of so he could attend a different school. (The school could also rescind the scholarship offer, but that rarely happens with top recruits.)

HOCKEY AND HIKING THE BALL

Oklahoma offensive coordinator Chuck Long liked hearing that Sam Bradford was a scratch golfer because golfers have to learn to get themselves out of jams and bounce back from bad breaks. Sam Bradford also believed his years of youth hockey weren't for naught, either.

"Hockey is so fast and unpredictable that it teaches you to think quickly and make snap decisions," Sam said. "I think that quality translates really well to playing quarterback."

He didn't mention checking, blocking, and blind side hits—another thing hockey and football have in common.

The Oklahoma coaches tendered the scholarship offer, and the Bradford family, as you can imagine, was thrilled that the Sooners—*their* Sooners!—wanted their son to play quarterback in Norman. But they didn't give an automatic yes. This was a big decision, and there was no reason to rush. Kent and Martha wanted to think things through with their son.

The family drove 20 miles south to the Oklahoma campus to meet with Long and head coach Bob Stoops. They had read all the hoopla in the newspapers about the pending arrival of Rhett Bomar, and they knew Oklahoma liked to stockpile extra quarterbacks—just in case things don't work out with the Big Recruit.

As the two sides hashed over the matter, Stoops and Long promised the Bradford family that Sam would be their only quarterback recruit in the 2006 class.

That was what the family wanted to hear. But there was something else Sam desired to get off his chest, and that was to declare his intentions to compete for playing time as soon as he arrived on campus. He wasn't going to take a back seat to anybody, including an ace like Rhett Bomar.

"If I come here, I'm coming to play," Sam said in a story recounted by Thayer Evans of the *New York Times*. Told by the Oklahoma coaches that the Sooners welcomed competition, Sam said, "Okay, that's all I wanted to know."

Everything was falling into place for the high school quarterback who had grown up in a bedroom that doubled as a shrine to Oklahoma Sooners football—mugs, pennants, banners, blankets, and other collectibles covered the walls, shelves, and dressers. He would be attending the college of his dreams, and his parents could easily watch him perform in the same 85,000-seat stadium where they had already made so many memories watching the Sooners play.

That's why Sam looked Coach Stoops and Coach Long in the eyes and said he was coming to Norman to play quarterback—not to hold a clipboard on the sideline.

SOONER DAYS

When Sam arrived at the Oklahoma campus in the summer of 2006, the Sooner football program was in turmoil.

Coach Stoops had just kicked quarterback Rhett Bomar and offensive guard J. D. Quinn off the team. The two had received money from Big Red Sports and Imports, a local car dealership, for doing work they—wink, wink—never performed. Apparently, the two never showed up to wash cars, even though they were clocked in.

"According to reports, Bomar had an arrangement with an OU-friendly car dealership that paid him thousands of dollars for performing little-to-no work," said *Sports Illustrated*'s Stewart Mandel. "It's the kind of thing so brazen in its stupidity that you wonder how on earth the involved parties thought they could get away with it."

Stoops said Bomar and Quinn "knowingly" broke the rules, and since they did so in an era of zero tolerance for violations of NCAA rules, they were dismissed from the team. You could say they were OUt of the picture.

Suddenly, the high school quarterback who was recruited almost as an afterthought had an opening.

Sam was coming off a solid senior year at Putnam North, but a porous offensive line, a lack of a threat at running back, and a sewn-up scholarship offer from Oklahoma painted a white bull's-eye on his cardinal and gold Panther jersey. Constantly harassed and chased from the pocket, Sam threw for "only" 2,029 yards and 17 touchdowns. When Putnam North failed to make the playoffs, some Sooners fans complained that Stoops had blown it when he promised to make Bradford the only quarterback in the 2006 recruiting class.

Welcome to the big leagues, Sam.

With Bomar gone, the Sooners faithful wondered if Stoops would plug the hole at quarterback with an untested true freshman—and eighteen years old, to boot. But the coach held firm and handed Sam his red shirt in training camp, meaning he wouldn't play during the 2006 season. This decision would preserve four years of eligibility, starting in 2007.

The Sooners didn't miss a beat, even with Paul Thompson, who had played wide receiver the previous season, in the quarterback role. Meanwhile, Sam handled the quarterback duties for the scout team during practice. All he could do during games was watch from the sideline, in street clothes, as the Sooners won the Big 12 title and a trip to the Fiesta Bowl, where they lost to Boise State. The Broncos scored on a two-point conversion play in overtime to win 43–42.

It practically killed Sam not to be playing. Remember, he'd been juggling three or four sports year-round for more than a decade, and he'd never been anything less than a key player on every team he was on. So when the start of the 2007 college football season rolled around, Sam wasn't about to spend another season watching someone else standing in the pocket—even if he *was* a redshirt freshman.

During summer training camp, Sam emerged from a three-way battle with sophomore Joey Halzle and first-year freshman Keith "Kid" Nichol to grab the reins of the Oklahoma team. Sam's sharp performances in several team scrimmages made the difference. In addition, the success of a "yearling" quarterback the previous year at the University of Texas—a redshirt freshman named Colt McCoy—increased the Oklahoma coaching staff's confidence that another red-shirt freshman was up to the job.

Kent Bradford was on cloud nine. "I just tried to teach him patience and probably play the role of the parent and offer him all the encouragement I could—'Hang in there, buddy,' that kind of thing," he said after learning his son had won the coveted position.

It didn't take long for Sam to prove to Sooners fans that Coach Stoops had made the right decision. In his debut, a home opener against the University of North Texas—a warm-up game, if you will—Sam completed 21 of 23 passes for 363 yards—all in a little over two quarters of work. The reason for the short day at the office: the Sooners won 79–10.

The following week, in a 51–13 home win over the University of Miami Hurricanes, Sam broke 2003 Heisman Trophy winner Jason White's school record for the most consecutive pass completions. The new number to beat: 23.

In the next two games—both big wins—the Sooners racked up 54 and 62 points to run their record to 4–0 and claw their way into the national title picture as the No. 4-ranked team in the nation.

Coach Stoops nicknamed Sam "The Big Easy" for his relaxed personality and unflappable attitude. Many of his teammates also said he was a calming influence in the huddle, no matter how well the offense was moving the ball. Then again, it helps when you're scoring on nearly every series.

Sportswriters noticed that Sam had thrown 25 touchdowns in the Sooners' first nine games, meaning he had a good chance to break the NCAA freshman record of 29 touchdown passes, set by David Neill of the University of

Nevada in 1988 and tied by a University of Texas quarterback named—you guessed it—Colt McCoy the year before.

The Sooners were on a roll, but a 27–24 road loss to Colorado in Boulder—after they had led 24–10 in the third quarter—came on a day when Sam had his first poor outing as the OU quarterback. His stats: 8-for-19 passing, 112 yards, one touchdown, and two interceptions.

With the loss, the Sooner bandwagon got caught in a wheel rut—but then Sam led the team on a five-game winning stampede, which included a Red River Rivalry (also known as the Red River Shootout) victory over the University of Texas.

The Red River Rivalry—which gets its name from the Red River, a natural boundary between Texas and Oklahoma—is an interstate game played every season at a "neutral" site—Dallas' Cotton Bowl, where Texas fans are allotted half the tickets and Sooners supporters take the other half.

Against Texas Tech, however, Oklahoma suffered its second loss of the season—and a major reason for the defeat was Sam's first serious injury. OU running back Allen Patrick lost a fumble, which Texas Tech linebacker Marlon Williams picked up. Sam chased after Williams to make a tackle, but he hit his head on the turf when he fell to the ground.

Sam returned for the next series, but when he came off the field, he couldn't remember any of the plays the team had run. He was done for the day, and so were the Sooners' hopes for a win.

Sam was cleared to play the next week in the Bedlam Game—the name for the annual contest against rival Oklahoma State—and he helped the Sooners deliver a sweet

49–17 rout of the Cowboys. Sweeter yet—at least on a personal level—was Sam's two-yard touchdown strike to tight end Joe Jon Finley during the second quarter, which broke the NCAA freshman record for TD passes in a season.

The victory over OSU put the Sooners into the Big 12 championship against the No. 1-ranked team in the country, Missouri. The Tigers' only loss of the season came earlier in the year to Oklahoma, so revenge, as well as a trip to the BCS Championship Game, was on their minds. Sam coolly denied Missouri a chance to play for the national championship, leading OU to a clear-cut 38–17 victory that sent the Sooners to Glendale, Arizona, for a January 2, 2008, matchup against West Virginia in the Fiesta Bowl.

The Mountaineers manhandled the Sooners, 48–28, however. Three sacks in the first half, plus several errant throws from Sam—including an interception—put Oklahoma in deep holes they couldn't dig their way out of. Still, in Sam's first season of college football, the Sooners finished the year ranked eighth in the nation with an 11–3 record, leaving him and Sooners fans believing all the pieces were in place for a run to the top in 2008.

After all, they had one of the nation's top-rated passers in their midst, and he was only going to get better.

BUILDING A HABITAT

They call it "team building."

A week before the start of training camp for the 2007 OU football season—before Sam had won the starting quarterback job—60 Sooners players stepped on a bus and traveled five miles south to Noble, Oklahoma, where the Christian charity Habitat for Humanity was building a house in a sleepy residential neighborhood. Sam Bradford, who had yet to don a red Sooners jersey in an official NCAA game, was on board in more ways than one.

This wasn't a 20-minute photo op for the six o'clock news. The beefy players put in a half-day's work in the stifling heat—a four-hour stretch of pounding nails, hefting lumber, and cleaning up the yard. The three OU quarterbacks—Sam, Joey Halzle, and Keith Nichol—drew weed duty.

Sam had learned the value of plugging into a ministry during his redshirt year in 2006. He arrived at the Oklahoma campus a bit untethered. It was his first time living away from home, of course, so there was that adjustment. Then the Rhett Bomar controversy blew up, which created an air of uncertainty. Remember, too, that Sam thought maybe he might get a chance to play right away as a true freshmen, but when Coach Stoops told Sam Oklahoma would redshirt him, he was thrown off kilter. Now he'd have to wait a whole year before he would have the opportunity to get in a real game.

Sam told CBN's Shawn Brown that his patience and perseverance were tested during his first semester in Norman. "I really struggled," he said. "I really struggled with the Lord because I came here and wasn't getting to play. I was sitting on the bench. I was having to wake up at 5 a.m. to go to workouts. That was a totally new concept to me. Every sport I'd played in, I always played. I never sat on the bench. So I kind of turned my back on the Lord. I was like, 'Why are You doing this to me? Why are You putting me in this situation?' "

Kent Bowles, the leader of the OU chapter of the Fellowship of Christian Athletes (FCA), checked in on the redshirt recruit. The FCA, which was founded in 1954 and is based in Kansas City, Missouri, is a nonprofit, interdenominational ministry that reaches out to young athletes and uses the powerful medium of athletics to impact the world for Jesus Christ.

Sam knew about the FCA because he was part of weekly "Huddle" meetings at Putnam North, which any student could attend. Huddles are where Christian fellowship and spiritual growth occur, but on the Oklahoma campus, Sam had yet to plug into the FCA or any other Christian fellowship group.

Bowles quietly but firmly challenged Sam about his relationship with Christ, saying he needed to get off the sidelines and into the game. Sam listened and got the message. A short time later, he began attending FCA meetings on campus and rekindled his relationship with Christ. He also struck up friendships with other Christians who could bolster him and pray for him.

SAM'S NEW PREGAME RITUAL

Moving ahead nearly a year later to the start of the 2007 season, the untested quarterback was nervous before the Sooners' first game against North Texas. Understandable, since 85,000 fans, including his parents, would be in the stands at Owen Field.

Even for home games, the Sooner team stayed in a hotel for meals and meetings. After the last meeting was over, he walked back to his hotel room and opened his Bible. He flipped some pages and landed in 1 Samuel 17, which tells the story of David and Goliath. He was mesmerized as he read about how David, a scrawny shepherd boy who had the fate of his people in his hands, took on a nine-foot-tall giant—a bruiser named Goliath.

The Bible says David wasn't afraid to take on a foe much taller, much heavier, and much more experienced. Instead, the rookie warrior used guile and his "throwing" skill when he raised his slingshot and whizzed a smooth stone with zip-line speed into the middle of Goliath's forehead. If the Israelites had ESPN *SportsCenter* replaying game highlights back then, the anchor would have praised David for delivering a courageous throw "between the numbers" . . . "when it mattered most" . . . "on the biggest stage" . . . "between two foes who don't like each other—the Philistines and the Israelites." You can see for yourself by reading the David and Goliath story from 1 Samuel 17.

Reading the against-all-odds story of David encouraged Sam and gave him the confidence he needed to take the field against North Texas. Afterward, he decided to make reading the David and Goliath story his pregame ritual throughout his college career at Oklahoma. (We'll see if he continues reading 1 Samuel 17 on Saturday nights or Sunday mornings when he starts playing for the Rams.)

ESPN's Ivan Maisel thinks he knows why Sam liked the David and Goliath story so much: "Bradford said it's not that he identifies with David, even though there are similarities. Like Bradford, David started as a freshman. And like Bradford, David led the FBS (First Book of Samuel) in passing efficiency—David completed his only attempt, a game-winner against favored Goliath."

Okay, we're just having some fun here, but there's a serious side to the David and Goliath story, which, after all, was a fight-to-the-death battle with huge implications for each side. First of all, David focused on God, not on the giant in his path. He could trust in the Lord because He was with him every step of the way. If he looked at giant problems and impossible situations from God's perspective, he could feel confidence in knowing God would fight for him and with him.

Emboldened *on* the field, Sam's spiritual confidence grew *off* the field. He became a fixture at the Tuesday night OU Huddle meetings, where he was "Sam"—just another guy who acted liked he wanted to be treated that way.

A Q&A WITH KENT BOWLES OF THE OKLAHOMA FCA

Is the story true that you checked in on Sam his freshman year and quietly but firmly challenged his relationship with Christ?

Kent: Sam was very approachable and easygoing. I just gently nudged him toward FCA, and he seemed excited to find a comfortable setting to plug into spiritually.

When did Sam start attending OU Huddle meetings?

Kent: Second semester of his redshirt freshman year. He attended regularly throughout his college career at Oklahoma, and he joined the FCA Leadership Team his sophomore year.

Where were the meetings held? Who attended them? Could anyone go?

Kent: The FCA meetings were held weekly in the athletic dining hall. We average about 100 students every meeting. Any student or student athlete could attend. We had mostly athletes attend at Oklahoma.

Is it true that Sam would either bring icebreaker games or do the icebreaker games? What were some of those icebreaker games?

Kent: Sam did what all of the other leaders did regularly. He opened in prayer, led games and icebreakers, introduced speakers, etc. Even though he garnered an enormous amount of attention on the field and in many circles of campus life, he was just another student athlete at FCA. Sam was old school. You could always count on him to lead an old-fashioned game of rock/scissors/paper!

What else did Sam contribute to the Huddles?

Kent: Sam made himself available to speak to the FCA Huddles in the Norman community. He also spoke to local churches as well. Sam made time in his schedule to be interviewed by FCA's *Sharing the Victory* magazine, which led to various media-related opportunities for FCA Huddles and students across the country.

What will Sam have to do to keep spiritually grounded in the NFL?

Kent: Sam makes great daily choices. Sam will continue to make those great decisions because he is grounded in his faith. Sam will not be enamored with fame and fortune. The spotlight is nothing new to him, and because he values faith and family, he will be a solid role model in the NFL.

The Three QBs come from solid, intact families, which unfortunately is not the norm these days. Talk about that.

Kent: I know that all three of these guys come from solid Christian families. That is rare these days. Sam has great parents who have raised him in a loving, Christian home.

The norm these days is to see about 6 of 10 athletes come from broken homes where the parents are divorced or never married. It certainly doesn't mean that kids from broken homes can't succeed and become solid in their faith and great Christian men and women. But the example of "family" is so important, and you can see the edge it gives a guy like Sam because it's just one element of life that is not a worry or a burden to overcome.

After the 2007 season, during the doldrums between the last bowl game and the start of spring practice, Coach Stoops dropped by the office of Kevin Wilson, who took over as OU offensive coordinator before the 2006 season. The topic turned to how the Sooners offense—already plenty potent during Sam's first season of college football—could score even *more* points.

Big 12 contests were becoming more like "track meets" than football games—with unstoppable offenses running and passing the ball up and down the field and racking up amazing scores. Unless your offense could keep up in this football version of the arms race, you could easily come out on the short end of a 49–42 score.

Stoops and Wilson both knew half the teams in the Big 12 were using a no-huddle offense—also known as the hurry-up offense—a type of strategy where the offense quickly gets to the line of scrimmage without huddling before running the next play.

Most teams use this strategy in the last two minutes of a half in order to get the ball downfield fast in a short amount of time. But more and more teams in the Big 12, and around the country, were utilizing a no-huddle offense *all* the time, meaning that as soon as the whistle blew the previous play dead, the offense was lining up in formation to start a new play. The quarterback then approached the center or stayed in the shotgun, but before starting the play count, he looked to his sideline for a signal for the next play. The quarterback then cupped his hands over his mouth and yelled out the play—all in coded numbers and phrases.

The no-huddle tires and disorients defenses, conserves

valuable clock time, and, from a fan's point of view, makes the game more exciting. Running the no-huddle takes tons of preparation and a quarterback who can process information on the fly and execute it flawlessly when the play starts.

Sam had led the nation in passing efficiency during his freshman season, so the Sooners had the right leader on the field.

Coach Wilson was on board. "If you want to run a no-huddle, I know how to do it," he told Stoops.

That spring, the OU coaches overhauled the offense, and what emerged was an up-tempo, fast-break offensive scheme that utilized multiple personnel groupings during the course of a game. The idea was to get the defense playing on its heels while Sam drilled receiver after receiver for 10- and 20-yard gains.

Although no one knew it at the time, Sam had just been handed the keys to a high-powered offense that would take Oklahoma to the BCS National Championship Game and propel him to the very top of college football's list of elite quarterbacks. The Sooners opened with 57, 52, and 55 points—against Chattanooga, Cincinnati, and Washington, respectively—and by early October they vaulted themselves to the top of the major college football polls as the No. 1 team in the country.

Even though the Sooners were running up tons of points and were at the top of the college football polls, Sam understood the importance of keeping their early-season success in perspective. "At this point, [it means] absolutely nothing," Sam said. "We've still got a way to go before we think about polls."

As the Sooners' prospects skyrocketed, the first whispers that Sam was worthy of consideration for the Heisman Trophy—the award given annually to the outstanding college football player whose performance best exhibits the pursuit of excellence with integrity—started appearing in the press. Sam, predictably, said he wasn't worried about individual awards, just about helping the team win.

The sixth game of the OU season—the Red River Rivalry—matched the unbeaten, top-ranked Sooners and the No. 5 Longhorns. ESPN's *College GameDay* analysts took turns saying, "This is a *big* game," and talked up the high-noon duel between a pair of Heisman Trophy candidates: Sam Bradford and Colt McCoy.

The Texas quarterback saw the Red River pairing as special. "How fun is it every week to be up against a team that has another great quarterback?" Colt said. "It's a challenge every week to know that, hey, there's another guy across the field that's leading his team and is playing really well. It makes it fun, it makes it exciting."

Even though Sam's and Colt's passing attempts and completions were nearly identical (Sam completed 28 of 39, while Colt was 28 of 35), Sam threw two interceptions, and Longhorn defense came up with the big stops in a 45–35 UT victory. The Oklahoma Sooners left Dallas that day sure that their BCS championship hopes had been dashed inside the Cotton Bowl.

Then something unexpected happened: Oklahoma's no-huddle offense went ballistic and Sam's passing blew the doors off the season. Check out these scores from the next six games:

- Oklahoma over Kansas State: 58–35
- Oklahoma over Nebraska: 62–28
- Oklahoma over Texas A&M: 66–28
- Oklahoma over Texas Tech: 65–21
- in the Bedlam Game, Oklahoma over Oklahoma State: 61–41
- in the Big 12 Championship game, Oklahoma over Missouri: 62–41

That season, the Sooners set a modern-day NCAA football record for scoring with 702 points, including at least 60 in each of their last five games. Hitler's tanks couldn't stop them. Defensive coordinators had trouble sleeping nights before games with Oklahoma. The nights after as well.

By virtue of winning the Big 12 and scoring in the 60s so often, the Sooners leapfrogged Texas and Florida in the national polls and grabbed the No. 1 spot. That development didn't sit well with Longhorns fans, whose Texas team beat Oklahoma back in October, but that's what the BCS computers spit out.

Oklahoma was back in the National Championship Game, this time against the University of Florida Gators at Dolphin Stadium in Miami.

The Gators had a great quarterback, too.

His name was Tim Tebow.

THE HEISMAN POSE

Two days after the Big 12 championship game, Sam underwent surgery to repair damaged ligaments in his non-throwing (left) hand, which he suffered during the Oklahoma State game. Coach Stoops told the media he expected Sam to be ready for the BCS Championship Game on January 8, 2009.

During the month-long wait, Sam learned he was a finalist for the Heisman Trophy, which would be awarded on December 13 at the Nokia Theatre in New York City. Two other quarterbacks were also invited to the televised event on ESPN: Colt McCoy, who had bounced back from a subpar sophomore season to put together a superlative junior year at Texas, and Tim Tebow, the Florida quarterback who the year before had become the youngest winner—and first sophomore ever—to win the Heisman Trophy.

Sam and his parents made their first trip together to the Big Apple to attend the Heisman ceremonies. The glare of the epicenter of the media universe was a bit overwhelming for Mom. "Sometimes," she said, her voice cracking, "you just have to pinch yourself and realize what's happening. It's just going so fast. I don't know if I'm taking it all in."

Inside the Nokia Theatre, the Heisman Trophy committee sat Sam, Tim, and Colt next to each other in the front row. The Three QBs, dressed in their Sunday best—jacket and tie—looked comfortable with the moment as previous Heisman winners were introduced and speeches were made.

Earlier, the three of them had sat in the green room together making small talk about their teams and the upcoming bowl games. They knew they were all Christians, so as the Heisman ceremony approached, they bowed their heads, clasped hands, and prayed that God would be glorified that evening. Since Tim had won the Heisman Trophy the year before, Sam asked him how it felt to be selected and what he might say should he win. "Don't forget to thank who was responsible," Tim replied.

When the announcement finally came, near the end of the hour-long event, Sam looked stunned when he heard his name spoken as the winner. He stood up, hugged Tebow and McCoy, then stepped a couple of rows back to grasp his beaming parents and Coach Stoops.

When Sam took the podium, his left hand in a cast covered with Sooners-red gauze, the first sentence out of his mouth was: "I first need to thank God. He has given me so many blessings, He's blessed me with so many opportunities, and He's put so many wonderful people in my life that I give all the credit to Him. Without Him, I'd be nowhere and we'd all be nowhere."

Just sixteen months after being named the starting quarterback at Oklahoma, Sam was the toast of college football as he clutched the illustrious bronze sculpture. He was the second sophomore—after Tim Tebow—to win the famed Heisman Trophy. In the second closest three-man race in the 73-year history of the award, Sam received 1,726 total points, edging out Colt (with 1,604 points) and Tim (with 1,575 points) to win the Heisman.

Kent and Martha Bradford, whose memory banks must have flashed through the hundreds of peewee ballgames and summer road trips to another weekend tournament, watched their son pose for pictures and sign autographs after the ESPN cameras had cut away.

"It's unbelievable," Martha said. "You can dream, but the Heisman . . . it's just on another planet."

Something else neat happened in New York during the Heisman event: Sam clicked with Colt. "I think we just got to talking," Sam said. "We were really similar in the way we were brought up. We both played a lot of sports growing up. I think we've gone through some of the same things. He started as a redshirt freshman. I started as a redshirt freshman."

Colt told Ivan Maisel of ESPN, "We both went to a small [high] school. We both really weren't recruited heavily out of high school. We both went to our in-state university that we loved and had grown up watching. He played all the sports in high school. So did I. We finally got to [high] school and focused on one thing, and that ended up being football."

FOR ALL THE MARBLES

The Bradford family hung around Manhattan a few more days after the Heisman ceremony while Sam made the media rounds, signed 300 footballs for the Heisman Trust, sat for his official Heisman portrait, rang the bell to begin trading at the New York Stock Exchange, and attended a formal Heisman banquet.

Meanwhile, winning the Heisman complicated Sam's life in some ways. Even though he had played only 27 games in a Sooners jersey, he was eligible for the NFL draft because he had spent the required three seasons in college, including his redshirt year. If Sam and the family decided the prudent thing for him to do would be to take the NFL's millions now (versus risking injury while playing another year of college football), they had to declare their intentions by January 15, 2009.

But first, there was another big game to play: the BCS Championship between the universities of Oklahoma and Florida, the top two teams in the country.

The Big 12 versus the Southeastern Conference.

Bob Stoops versus Urban Meyer.

Sam Bradford versus Tim Tebow.

The day after Sam cradled the Heisman Trophy, Jeremy Fowler of *The Orlando Sentinel* laid down a Gator gauntlet when he wrote, "His smirk said he got robbed. His body language said he's going to make Oklahoma feel that pain on January 8 in the national title game."

Fowler was referring, of course, to Tim Tebow, who won the most *first-place* votes in the complicated Heisman voting procedure but still finished a close third. An analysis showed that Tebow took his biggest hit from voters in the Southwest region, which included those from Oklahoma and Texas—folks who would be expected to be "Florida haters." The Heisman snub, Fowler believed, would fuel the fire in Tebow's belly.

The trash talk began when Sooners cornerback Dominique Franks said before the game that if Tim Tebow played in the Big 12, he'd "probably be about the fourth-best quarterback in our conference."

Reporters rushed to Tim's side to ask him if he believed he would *really* be the fourth-best quarterback in the Big 12, which prompted a laugh and a wise "I don't really need to talk about that." Florida linebacker Brandon Spikes, however, couldn't resist the microphone, calling Big 12 defenses "a joke" and saying that when he watches ESPN *SportsCenter*, "I look at the scores, and it's 56–49, just basketball scores."

Oklahoma came into the BCS Championship Game with a 12–1 record and ranked No. 1, while Florida, also 12–1, was ranked No. 2. "Clash of the Titans" was the way the game was billed, a marquee match-up pitting the unstoppable Sooners offense against the Gators' stiff defense.

Dolphin Stadium was crammed with 78,468 fans, and they watched as the Sooner offense failed to score on several early opportunities. Sometimes OU just stalled and sometimes penalties and mental mistakes stopped the team. The Gators stuffed the Sooners on a fourth-and-goal from the one-yard line, and then, on the six-yard line, with 10 seconds to go in the first half, Sam forced a throw into coverage. The Florida defense tipped and intercepted the pass at the goal line.

The game remained close, though. Early in the fourth quarter, with Florida leading 17–14, Sam was driving his team toward a possible touchdown, and the lead, when the key play of the game took place. Florida defensive back Ahmad Black wrestled the ball out of the hands of Sooners receiver Juaquin Iglesias, who was on a deep pass route. Suddenly, Tim Tebow and the Gators smelled victory, and they embarked on an 11-play, 76-yard scoring drive that took 6:52 off the clock, essentially sealing the game for Florida.

Tebow, who bounced back from a couple of first-half interceptions, was clearly on a mission. Throughout the game, he lowered his shoulder and plowed his way through the Sooner defense. One time he cracked an OU linebacker with a meaty forearm. He executed a nifty "jump pass" late in the fourth quarter to clinch the victory and claim the Gators' second national championship in three seasons and third overall.

"You don't want to wake up a sleeping giant," said Florida running back Percy Harvin after the game.

Sam knew his performance was subpar. "In the second

half, when we needed to make plays, we just couldn't do it," he said.

Six days later, back in Norman, Sam announced he would return for his junior year at Oklahoma. The loss to Florida played a "little bit" into his decision, but what he really didn't want to do was cut short his college experience at Oklahoma. There was some unfinished business, and that was bringing home the Sooners' eighth national championship.

But then the game of life would take an unexpected bounce for Sam Bradford.

RISKY BUSINESS

When Sam opted to return for his junior year, Kent Bradford knew his son was taking a calculated risk. A serious injury— even a career-ending one—was always just one play away.

Kent also knew something about insurance policies. As the president of Bradford-Irwin Insurance, that was his business. Although he specialized in commercial insurance, his knowledge of the industry proved invaluable as he researched the types of "doomsday" policies that were out there for his son. They all came with exclusions written in favor of the insurance companies, as well as coverage triggers and rehab requirements, so you had to know what you were doing. Cost of a $2 million policy in the event of a career-ending injury: a hefty $20,000 a year.

Kent declined to state how much insurance the family took out on Sam, but it's worth noting that the families of Colt McCoy and Tim Tebow were thinking along the same lines. The McCoy family purchased a policy for Colt that ranged from $3 million to $5 million, and Tim's was worth an estimated $2 million.

Maybe Kent sensed they would need the insurance policy in their hip pocket, or maybe he likes to sleep better at night.

The first omen that things were going to go south for Sam Bradford and the Sooners took place in training camp, when All-American tight end Jermaine Gresham suffered a knee injury and was lost before the season even began. Also, the offensive line never got settled, and in the season opener against Brigham Young, the inexperienced line committed 12 penalties, missed several blocking assignments, and failed to keep the BYU defensive lineman and linebackers from racing into the Sooner backfield. When Sam stepped back to pass, he never knew if he would have to run for his life or get the ball off before he wanted to.

On one key play, a blitzing BYU linebacker found a free lane and delivered a devastating hit on Sam, slamming him into the turf and knocking him out of the game with a sprained acromioclavicular (AC) joint in the shoulder of his throwing arm. There was no damage to the collar bone, rotator cuff, or ball and socket, but Sam would be out two to four weeks.

His new BFF, Colt McCoy, sent him a text message wishing him a speedy recovery. Colt wanted Sam to recover quickly since the pair had a rematch coming up in a month: Oklahoma versus Texas in the Red River Rivalry at the Cotton Bowl.

With pressure mounting to get back on the field, Sam returned three weeks later to lead a lopsided win over Baylor. Then it was on to Dallas. This time around, the 20th-ranked

Sooners were coming in as clear underdogs to the No. 3 Longhorns.

Sam started the Red River Rivalry game, but he wasn't able to finish it. During Oklahoma's second series, speedy Longhorns cornerback Aaron Williams blitzed untouched from the right side and smothered Sam—right on his bum shoulder. For the second time in a month, the Oklahoma quarterback writhed in pain, even falling to his knees. Sam Bradford's junior season was over.

A few days later, Sam announced he would submit to season-ending surgery to repair damaged ligaments in his throwing shoulder. Dr. James Andrews, a renowned sports orthopedic surgeon in Birmingham, Alabama—where many of the pros go when they want the best treatment available—would be performing the operation.

Before traveling to Alabama, Sam dropped by the Sooners' locker room to say good-bye to his teammates, thank his coaches, and conduct a farewell press conference. One of the first questions asked was whether he had any regrets about deciding to return to the University of Oklahoma for the 2009 season.

"No," he shot back. "Absolutely 100 percent no regrets."

He expanded on that thought: "Considering this is where I grew up and this is where I dreamed of playing, to put this in the past is extremely tough. I've been blessed to be here. The past three and a half years have been the best three and a half years of my life. I wouldn't trade a day of it."

In Birmingham, Kent was allowed to witness part of Dr. Andrews' 35-minute procedure on Sam's shoulder, which was termed successful. Later, to the surprise of no one, the family announced that Sam would forego his senior year at OU and make himself available for the NFL draft in April.

Still, the questions remained. Would the shoulder injury cost Sam millions of dollars? Was he "damaged goods" as far as the NFL was concerned? No one would know the answers to those questions until four to five months of rehabilitation had passed.

One thing was certain, though: the last thing the Bradfords wanted to do was cash in on that insurance policy.

2

COLT MCCOY:
THE EYES OF TEXAS ARE UPON HIM

The last time we saw Colt McCoy in a college football uniform, he was standing on the floor of the Rose Bowl, grasping
his jersey and shoulder pads with his left hand while ABC's
sideline reporter Lisa Salters cocked a microphone below his
chin.

Behind him, joyous University of Alabama players danced
jigs of celebration while tens of thousands of Crimson Tide
fans in attendance reveled in their school's first national
championship since 1992. Alabama had beaten the proud
University of Texas Longhorns 37–21 in the BCS National
Championship Game, held on January 7, 2010.

A blank look of dejection covered Colt's face. The moment he had worked for his entire college football career had
slipped through his fingers like a muddy football.

Coming into the game, Colt was in top shape. He had
done the necessary work on the practice field and in the

weight room. He had spent the month of December studying film for one game against the Crimson Tide. He was ready to lead his No. 2-ranked team to a BCS national championship.

But all his preparation and hard work were taken away in one play.

Shortly after the opening kickoff, Texas safety Blake Gideon intercepted an ill-advised throw on a fake punt, and the Longhorns were in business on the Alabama 37-yard line. Colt quickly moved the Texas offense to the 11-yard line, and on the fifth play of the drive, he took the snap and darted to his left. This was an option play in which he had the choice of flipping the football to his trailing tailback, Tre' Newton, or running the ball into the end zone himself if he saw daylight.

Alabama's sturdy defensive tackle Marcel Dareus, however, slid off a block and jolted Colt, knocking him onto the back of Texas center Chris Hall. The collision didn't look like anything out of the ordinary, but, as ABC color commentator Kirk Herbstreit said during a replay, Marcel Dareus "is 300 pounds coming downhill in a hurry."

Colt didn't waste any time getting back to his feet, but as he got his bearings, he rotated his right shoulder and started jogging toward the Texas sideline. With his left arm, he motioned for someone to replace him while his right arm hung to his side, limp as a flag in still air.

Trainers huddled with Colt on the sideline before escorting him to the Texas locker room, located in the corner of the end zone. His father, Brad McCoy, a Texas high school football coach who had nurtured Colt's football career from day one, left his seat and headed to the bowels of the Rose

Bowl to comfort his oldest son.

Brad watched Colt take off his predominantly white Longhorn jersey and shoulder pads and lie down on a table for X-rays. The film was quickly developed, and team doctors peered at the images against a lighted background. "Negative," they agreed. Nothing in his right shoulder was fractured.

Their diagnosis made sense to Colt. The shoulder didn't hurt—but he couldn't feel his arm. Trainers applied bags of ice to the shoulder to stop any inflammation.

Colt pleaded with the team doctors and trainers to return to the game. *I can play. Let me go in. Just give me a chance. My arm is okay.*

Colt had fibbed, and he admitted as much afterwards. His arm wasn't okay. The limb felt dead—like he had slept on it all night and just woke up. But his heart was willing. He desperately wanted to play, and his team needed him. From a TV set hanging in a corner of the locker room, everyone could see that Alabama was starting to run away with the game in the second quarter.

Okay, let's see you throw, one of the trainers said.

Inside the Rose Bowl locker room, Colt lined up just seven yards away from his father. How many passes had father and son lobbed back and forth to each other over the years? It seemed like millions to Colt. He was just a toddler when they started playing catch in the backyard of their home. With the passage of time, they moved to the football field of Jim Ned High School in tiny Tuscola, Texas, where the father was the coach and the son became the star quarterback.

Inside the Rose Bowl locker room, however, Colt threw. . . well, like a girl. Nothing on the ball. Afterward, he said his arm felt like a "wet noodle."

The Texas medical personnel shook their heads. *We can't let you play, son.* They explained that he had suffered a pinched nerve in his shoulder—also known as a "stinger" or "burner"—following the violent collision with Dareus. He most likely wouldn't require surgery, but the normal course of treatment was three weeks of rest and rehabilitation.

Colt McCoy's career as a Longhorn was over.

The quarterback who had started every game for Texas over the past four seasons—the ironman who never got hurt—was knocked out of his final game in what should have been the fitting climax to his college football career.

This wasn't the storybook ending Colt had dreamed about. He was supposed to lead the Longhorns of the University of Texas—*his* team—to a BCS national championship, just like another Texas quarterback, Vince Young, had done four years and three days earlier on the same Rose Bowl turf—when Colt was a redshirt noncombatant for the 2006 BCS Championship Game.

During a lull in that game's action, Young approached the kid holding a clipboard. "You need to watch," the celebrated Texas quarterback said. "This is going to be you."

Colt nervously paced the Texas sidelines as the Longhorns, down 38–33, had one last chance to come from behind and snatch victory from the USC Trojans. The game hung in the balance when the Texas offense faced a fourth-and-five from the 8-yard line with less than 30 seconds to go.

Fail to convert, and game over.

Any Longhorn fan can tell you what happened next. Vince Young took the snap, scanned the field, and went through his progressions, but he couldn't find an open receiver. With the screams of 93,986 fans ringing in his ears, Young took off on a diagonal for the right pylon of the end zone, and, in a foot-race, beat the Trojan linebackers to the goal line. Bedlam—and an improbable come-from-behind victory and national championship for the University of Texas.

Tonight was Colt's moment on the same stage, in the same stadium, and with the same stakes—finishing the season as the No. 1 team in college football. It was Texas versus Alabama for the American Football Coaches Association (AFCA) trophy and a chance to hoist an eight-pound Waterford crystal football above his head. But after taking the shot to his right shoulder early in the game, Colt could barely toss a football across a room to his father.

His teammates would have to win without him.

One of the team doctors instructed him to take a shower and watch the second half in team sweats. Colt ignored the directive and put his pads back on, just in case feeling and strength returned to his arm. If he couldn't play, he decided, then he would at least be the team leader he had always been, encouraging his teammates to never give up and helping out where he could.

The second quarter ended, and a downcast Texas team trudged to the locker room, where they found Colt waiting for them. His replacement at quarterback, Garrett Gilbert—the true freshman who saw only mop-up duty behind Colt during the regular season—looked like a ghost. His play had been a train wreck. After the Texas coaches had ordered him to get in there and replace Colt, he couldn't find his helmet. He rushed throws and frequently bounced passes to his receivers. He looked uncomfortable and out of his element. During the first half, he completed three passes out of 10 throws—with Alabama players making two of those catches.

The last interception took place with 15 seconds to go in the first half, when Marcel Dareus—him again!—deflected and corralled Gilbert's short shovel pass. The beefy 'Bama player rumbled for the end zone, shoving Gilbert aside like he was a rag doll. No wonder Gilbert looked down and depressed as he entered the locker room. Alabama had a huge 24–6 lead at intermission.

"Stay calm out there," Colt counseled Gilbert. "Keep your head up. Keep plugging away and something good is going to happen."

Colt, still in full pads and uniform, returned to the sidelines after halftime and wore a headset to stay involved with the play-calling. Between offensive series, he tutored Gilbert like the freshman quarterback he was.

Something clicked in the second half. The inexperienced quarterback who had lost his way in the first half mounted an improbable comeback. Two well-thrown touchdown passes cut the 24–6 deficit to 24–21 with 6:15 to go in the fourth quarter. A last-gasp effort, however, failed when Gilbert was pressured and fumbled, leading to another Tide touchdown.

That was the game.

When Alabama ran out the clock and the victorious players in red jerseys began rejoicing their victory, ABC's Lisa Salters and a cameraman chased after Colt to get his reaction. With the camera's red light turned on and millions of TV sets tuned in, Ms. Salters asked him, "What was it like for you to watch this game—the last game in uniform—from a sideline?"

Instead of a glib reply or falling back on the typical jock clichés, Colt ruefully shook his head. *Twice* he began, "I . . . I . . ." before stopping to regroup. Then he look another long, long moment—an eternity on live TV—to gather himself. It was clear he was fighting his emotions.

Perhaps he was remembering what happened the night before with Jordan Shipley, his best friend, roommate, and wide receiver on the Texas team. On the eve of the Rose Bowl game, they sat in their hotel room and read Isaiah 26:4: "Trust in the LORD always, for the LORD GOD is the eternal Rock" (New Living Translation).

Just when it looked like he had lost his voice—or his nerve—Colt called his own number. "I . . . I love this game," he began in his slight but distinctive Texas twang. "I have a passion for this game. I've done everything I can to contribute to my team, and we made it this far. It's unfortunate that I didn't get to play. I would have given everything I had to be out there with my team. Congratulations to Alabama. I love the way our team fought. Garrett Gilbert stepped in and played as good as he could play. He did a tremendous job. I always give God the glory. I never question why things happen the way they do. God is in control of my life, and I know that . . . I am standing on the Rock."

In addition to his articulateness with the entire sporting nation looking in, the greatest thing about Colt's response was his expression. His face carried an angelic look of happiness and assurance of who he was, in victory or defeat.

In many ways, he was just as ready for this trying moment as he would have been for a Texas victory.

WATCH FOR YOURSELF

If you've never seen Colt's postgame interview with Lisa Salters, or would like to revisit the experience, all it takes is a few minutes to watch online. You can find numerous versions on YouTube by typing in "Colt McCoy Rose Bowl 2010 interview." But perhaps the best viewing experience comes from ESPN. The link is: http://espn.go.com/blog/sportscenter/tag/_/name/lisa-salters

BORN ON TEXAS SOIL

The name Colt McCoy is pure Texan and sounds like a movie character from a 1940s rootin'-tootin' western featuring Colt, who'd insist on playing the role of the gunslinger in a white hat. To carry the Wild West theme a step further, if Sam Bradford has a cannon of an arm, then Colt has a deadly accurate rifle.

In 2008 Colt completed 77.6 percent of his passes to set a new NCAA record for highest single-season completion percentage. He also won more games (45) than any other starting quarterback in NCAA history, and though he never won the Heisman Trophy like Sam Bradford and Tim Tebow did, he played in—and started—more games (53) than either Sam or Tim.

Daniel Colt McCoy was born on September 5, 1986, making him the eldest of the Three QBs. He's nearly a year older than Tim Tebow and fifteen months older than Sam Bradford, and he was a grade ahead in high school.

Colt's parents named him after the Old Testament prophet, but if you ever meet him, don't call him Daniel—or Dan.

He *hates* his given name and has gone by Colt all his life, which is why offensive linemen at Texas constantly called him Daniel.

That's not the only way the Longhorn linemen liked to tease Colt. "They also like to torture him by pretending to punch him in the man region before pulling up inches short," wrote Rick Reilly, the hilarious ESPN.com columnist. "If McCoy flinches, they get to slug him hard twice in the shoulder [author's note: it had better be his *left* shoulder], then 'wipe' off these slugs, which means taking one of their meaty hands and wiping it down McCoy's face, in his eyes, up his nostrils, and into his mouth."

Football players love these kinds of silly games, even in the huddle. "I'll be trying to call a play, and one of those guys is sticking his big ol' fingers up my nose. I get no respect," he said.

Colt has been around these types of football hijinks for as long as he can remember because he's the son of a high school football coach. His father, Brad McCoy, got into coaching after playing football at Abilene Christian University in Abilene, Texas.

Colt's father was merely following in the footsteps of *his* father, Burl, a football star at ACU who later became the school's women's basketball coach. Good thing Colt's grandfather moved into basketball. Why? Because you could say Burl recruited Brad's wife.

The story goes that Colt's mom, Debra, had been attending Harding University in Arkansas. She really wanted to play basketball, so she transferred to ACU to play on Burl McCoy's team. One day, Brad dropped by Moody Coliseum when his eyes caught sight of a beautiful young woman bouncing a basketball. He turned to a friend and said, "I don't even know that girl, but I'm going to marry her."

Debra rebuffed Brad's first overtures to go out, but she relented when *she* asked *him* to be her date at a Sadie Hawkins dance. Brad and Debra were an item after that, and Debra went on to capture all-conference honors on the basketball court.

Brad was a wide receiver at Abilene Christian in the early 1980s, where his roommate was running back Bob Shipley. (Don't forget that name.) They became very close friends and talked about everything, from football to their love interests. Bob was dating Sharon Felts, the daughter of Addie Felts, Abilene Christian's first women's track coach, so it seemed like everything was happening in the ACU family.

Following graduation, Brad married Debra and Bob married Sharon, and the two men set off to become high school football coaches. Brad started at just about the lowest rung on the coaching ladder: assistant coach at Lovington High School in Lovington, New Mexico. It wasn't Texas high school football and *Friday Night Lights*, but it was a start.

TRIVIA TIME

Brad McCoy has already coached one player to the NFL. Brian Urlacher, the Chicago Bears linebacker, played for him at Lovington High in the mid-1990s. They have remained good friends, and Brad worked for several years at Urlacher's summer football camp in Albuquerque. The Chicago Bears star has also visited the McCoy family in Texas.

BORN IN TEXAS . . . SORT OF

Lovington, a small city of 10,000 located 17 miles west of the Texas border, is known as the Queen City of the Plains. The main regional hospital, however, was in Hobbs, 20 miles to the southeast, which was fine with Brad McCoy since Hobbs was even closer to Texas—just five miles from the border. This was significant, as you will see.

But five miles is five miles, and Hobbs will always be part of New Mexico. After Debra went through labor and delivered Colt, the infant boy was gingerly placed in a hospital crib. According to a Texas tall tale, Brad drove five miles to the Texas border, where he scooped several handfuls of Lone Star dirt into a shoebox. Then he returned to the hospital, where he placed the cardboard box of Texas red earth underneath Colt's bassinet. He did this because he wanted to tell his family back home that Colt was born on Texas soil.

This story has been repeated so often that it's taken a life of its own. When Brad was asked to confirm this fable, he smiled and said, "I plead the Fifth," referring to the amendment to the U.S. Constitution that protects him from making self-incriminating statements. Colt was also asked about the "shoebox of Texas dirt" story, but he sidestepped the question as neatly as he evades a blitzing linebacker. "I can't remember," he said. "I was a little baby. That's what my folks say. Nobody's said it wasn't true, so I guess it's true."

With a father as a football coach, you can figure Colt hung around plenty of grassy fields as a preschooler, shagging balls and playing imaginary games. He was probably adopted as the team mascot at times.

When Colt started elementary school, his father would

drop him off and say the same two things every morning:

"I love you."

And:

"Do your best and be a leader."

The fatherly advice became a game. Whenever Colt would reach for the car door, his father would remind that he loved him. "Do your best—"

"—and be a leader," Colt would reply as he slammed the door shut.

Brad had decided he and Debra would raise Colt—and his younger brothers Chance and Case (born two and five years after Colt, respectively)—according to four godly principles:

1. They would prepare their children for the path, not the path for their children. The road is rough, narrow, and hard to find, but God had given them a roadmap—the Bible. They could prepare their children for the future by remembering Proverbs 22:6: "Train a child in the way he should go, and when he is old he will not turn from it." They couldn't overlook authority and order, which is found in Proverbs 23:13: "Do not withhold discipline from a child; if you punish him with the rod, he will not die."

2. They would prepare their children to be the best. This is why Brad reminded Colt each morning to "do your best and be a leader." Sure, when Colt and his brothers got older, they responded with the typical *Yeah, Dad, we know,* but Brad would always lead his football teams onto the field with the chant, "Expect to win, play to win."

Parents should also aim high, not low. The applicable Scripture is 1 Corinthians 9:24: "Do you not know that in a race all the runners run, but only one gets the prize? Run in such a way as to get the prize."

3. They would prepare their children to be leaders. It's not enough to be the best, but their children had to learn how to lead as well.

4. They would prepare their children for open and closed doors. Brad and Debra knew they had to trust the Lord in whatever happens in the lives of their children. Some doors will open, and some will close, but God knows what's best and has a plan for their lives.

Brad says he raised Colt and his brothers in a disciplined home. "We're fundamental," he said. "You go to bed early, get up early, and take care of your body. We're a churchgoing family. Sunday morning is Sunday morning, and we go to church. If we couldn't give back a couple of hours on the Lord's Day, then something's wrong. As they [Colt, Chance, and Case] got older, they've understood the importance of that aspect, and I think that's really strengthened them as young men."

ONLY MIDDLE NAMES, PLEASE

If you're thinking that Chance and Case are out-of-the-ordinary first names, you should know that Colt's brothers go by their middle names as well.

SIDELINE PASS

One of Colt's earliest football memories was an incident that took place when he was four years old. He had been named the official water boy for one Friday night game, and he was

standing on the Lovington High sidelines when one of the players ran out of bounds and squashed the pint-sized Colt, knocking him flat. Result: a horrific scream and a broken collarbone.

Colt learned to keep his eyes on the field after that.

The youngster was promoted to ball boy when he hit his
elementary school years. Colt loved watching the gargantuan
gladiators in helmets and pads slug it out. One time, when he
was eight years old, Lovington High was mounting a drive.
Colt tugged on his father's pants leg. "Dad, if you run a screen
now, it'll work," said the third grader.

His father signaled in the play for a screen pass—touchdown!

"Yeah, that happened," Brad said. "Absolutely true."

By the time he was twelve, Colt was already helping his
father break down game film and learning the intricacies of
the game. The summer before Colt's seventh-grade year, Brad
asked his son, who had already played several seasons of peewee football at the quarterback position, if he was ready to
dedicate himself to something—like becoming a better football player.

As they talked about what he could do to better himself,
Colt mentioned that a speaker came to his middle school and
challenged the students to live healthy lifestyles. "Athletes do
not drink sodas," the health speaker said. "Soda slows you
down."

So father and son talked about Colt's Dr Pepper habit.
Known as the "national drink of Texas," Dr Pepper's unique
flavor was created in Waco in 1885 and was practically the
beverage of choice in the Southwest. Colt was drinking at
least a six-pack a day of the heavily sugared and carbonated

soft drink, which contained 54 grams of sugar and 200 calories in each 16-ounce bottle. By drinking six bottles of Dr Pepper, Colt's young, growing body was consuming 1,200 nutritionless calories a day and enough sugar to keep a classroom of kindergartners on hyper-alert all afternoon.

"We were at On the Border by Six Flags in Arlington," Brad said. "He drank a Dr Pepper then and said, 'That's the last one of those I'm ever going to drink. I'll be a better athlete if I don't drink that stuff anymore.'"

That event happened 10 years before Colt's senior season at the University of Texas, and Colt hasn't sipped a Dr Pepper or soft drink since—which has to be difficult, especially since his friends and peers surely drink soda pop like it's coming out of a drinking fountain. But Colt hasn't wavered; he's been a water, milk, and Gatorade guy ever since. (Irony time: when Colt played at Texas, Dr Pepper was the official drink of the Big 12 Conference.)

SMALL TOWN VALUES

During his middle school years, Colt showed every sign that he would become an excellent athlete. "A guy told me after the third game Colt played as a seventh grader that he was going to win the Heisman one day," Brad said. "I just laughed and told him he was crazy. But it was obviously noticeable that he had a lot of special characteristics."

Meanwhile, the family moved back to Texas as Brad took coaching positions at small schools in San Saba and Kermit. The coach could have moved into a big-time high school program in Dallas or Houston, but he and Debra didn't want to raise their sons in a metropolitan city or leafy suburb. They preferred one-stoplight towns in the proverbial middle-of-nowhere, places where everyone knew each other's name. This was the family-friendly atmosphere in which they sought to raise their sons. Hunting and fishing were their passions.

"I caught some criticism for it," Brad said, "but it's a choice I'm comfortable with. I enjoy the slow pace. I like knowing who my kids are hanging out with. It's a lifestyle that suits our family just fine."

That lifestyle included frequent trips to see family and friends around the great state of Texas. Since coaches and teachers receive the same school holidays and summer breaks as students, there was plenty of time to hunt and fish at Grandpa Burl's ranch south of Abilene, as well as vacation with their best friends—the Shipleys.

COLT MCCOY, GOSPEL SINGER

In the late 1970s, Burl McCoy started an a cappella gospel group called the McCoy Family Singers. The group is comprised of Colt's grandparents (Burl and Jan), his father, Brad, and two of his father's siblings, Uncle Michael and Aunt Amy. They are the Texas version of the von Trapp family: throughout the last three decades, the McCoy Family Singers have performed in front of thousands and released 11 albums.

The group sings without instruments because, as members of the Church of Christ denomination, they hold to a doctrinal tenet that the only musical instrument God created was the human voice; man created the rest.

One of the McCoy Family Singers albums, a 2008 release named *I Will Give Thanks*, is available on iTunes. Rumor has it that Colt sang on a couple of recordings.

Bob Shipley, Brad's roommate back in their college days, was putting together a successful high school football coaching career as well. When the kids started coming along, the two families made time to go to church camp together or pitch tents at Devils River in southwest Texas, where nothing more strenuous than fishing, reading, and hanging out was on the agenda.

The Shipleys' oldest child, Jordan, was nine months older than Colt, and the two were inseparable. They were always competing: who could catch the biggest fish, bag the biggest deer, or win at H-O-R-S-E in basketball. They practiced their football skills, too. Jordan would run pass routes until his tongue hung out so Colt could fine-tune his timing and accuracy.

In the late 1990s, the two families lived within 20 miles of each other in the Big Country communities of Hamlin and Rotan, north of Abilene. Brad had taken a coaching job at Hamlin High; Bob was coaching at Rotan.

Then, during Colt's middle school years, the McCoy family moved to Tuscola (pronounced TUSS-koh-lah), a central Texas farming town in Taylor County that's located 20 miles south of Abilene and 200 miles west of Dallas. The population posted on U.S. Highway 83 coming into town was 714—Babe Ruth's career home run number—with 202 families residing within the town's limits. Brad was hired as the head football coach for Jim Ned High School in Tuscola, and he and Debra purchased a ranch house outside town. Ten acres of peace and quiet. Room for their animals to roam. No noisy neighbors. A blanket of stars each night.

Tuscola wasn't even a one-stoplight town. A blinking

yellow light controlled the main intersection of U.S. 83 and Graham Street, where a convenience store/café was situated. You could find an American Legion Hall, a funeral home, a volunteer fire department, a couple of banks, a post office, a florist shop, a handful of restaurants, 10 churches, and a water tower. That's all you need, right? Well, the locals would tell you the only thing missing was a Dairy Queen.

Tuscola's major industries were cotton, wheat, cattle, and high school football, and this is where Brad came in. Jim Ned High School—named after a nineteenth-century Indian cavalry scout for the U.S. Army—educated about 330 students drawn from a school district that covered 380 square miles. The football team competed in the 2A division of Texas high school athletics and was the biggest game in town.

The move to Tuscola—actually, the McCoys lived closer to a town called Buffalo Gap, population 463—checked off a lot of boxes for Brad and Debra. They still maintained the small-town atmosphere they had enjoyed in Hamlin—although the family joked that they had to go *into* town to hunt since they lived so far from Tuscola's main drag. The move placed them closer to Burl McCoy's ranch south of Abilene. And they could worship in Abilene at the Oldham Lane Church of Christ, which had been the McCoy's denomination for several generations.

Little did the residents of Tuscola know that Colt McCoy would put this tiny Texas town on the map—or that Colt's favorite teacher at Jim Ned High, Kay Whitton, would one day attend University of Texas games carrying a homemade sign that read:

TUSCOLTA, POP. 714

THE JIM NED YEARS

Vince Lavallee, the assistant football coach and vice principal at Jim Ned, remembers the time Colt jogged off the field at Coahoma High and a young fan thrust a piece of paper and a pen in front of the young quarterback.

"Can I have your autograph?" the fan asked.

The year was 2002. Colt was a sophomore in high school. No one had ever asked him for an autograph before. He turned and looked to his assistant coach for advice. "What do I do?" he asked.

"Sign it," Lavallee replied. "It'll probably be the first of many."

No one doubted—or gossiped about—Brad McCoy's decision to play his son at quarterback during his first season of high school football. Even as a sophomore, Colt overwhelmed the competition, but that's the beauty of playing at the 2A level. With such a small pool of talent to draw from, a great athlete like Colt stood out like a prize steer in a cattle herd.

Another aspect of small school football is that the superior athletes play on offense *and* defense—it's called "going both ways." Coach McCoy needed some help in the defensive backfield, so he played Colt at free safety. Late in the season, however, when 8–0 Jim Ned played Bangs High School, Bangs' 215-pound running back Jacoby Jones (who later played at Baylor University) turned the corner and ran upfield. Colt, the last line of defense, threw his body in front of the powerful runner and suffered a concussion.

Colt was held out of the next two games, which unraveled Jim Ned High School's aspirations for a state championship.

His father, being the smart coach that he is, never played Colt on defense again.

But word got around about the kid with a rifle arm, and during Colt's junior year of high school, Jim Ned's stadium bleachers were filled with football fans from Ovalo, Lawn, Goldsboro, and Novice. They wanted to see what this McCoy kid was all about. He wore No. 4—the same jersey number as another quarterback putting up impressive numbers: Brett Favre of the Green Bay Packers.

Like Sam Bradford, Colt had his best—or most success-ful—high school season as a junior. Now that he no longer played defense, Colt helped out the team by taking on the punting duties. He had a good leg, too, averaging about 37 yards a kick (by comparison, college and pros average around 43 to 45 yards per punt).

With Colt at the reins, a pass-happy offense gobbled up yards in chunks, and Jim Ned advanced to the Texas State 2A championship game in Dallas with a perfect 14–0 record. The Indians, however, were trounced decisively by San Augus-tine, 28–7—the first time since Colt started playing middle school football that his team has gone down to defeat with him shouldering the quarterbacking duties.

"We got beat on a cold night in Dallas," his father said. "I remember he was at midfield sobbing, and I really felt like it was too much, so I picked him up and said I understand it was a state championship game and all. With tears rolling from his eyes, he stopped me and said, 'You don't understand. This is the first I've ever stood on a football field after a game that I've lost.' That was his mentality."

Despite Colt's suffering his first defeat, word was getting

around about this phenom from the Texas prairie who was All-State at the Class 2A level. Fifty touchdowns in 15 games, 3,939 yards, and only 11 interceptions during his junior season got him on the recruiting boards.

That, however, didn't mean there was a stampede of college coaches rushing into Tuscola. Remember, Jim Ned High School was a small school competing at the 2A level, and there were three higher divisions (3A, 4A, and 5A) in Texas high school football. That's why there were questions about whether Colt could compete against players who were taller, faster, and heavier. Plus Colt was on the smallish side—probably a little over six feet and a buck-seventy in weight—despite being officially "listed" at 6 feet, 2½ inches tall and weighing 188 pounds.

But Colt sure looked good on film, and his pinpoint passing earned him a second look with college coaches. Even though Tuscola was in Texas Tech territory, there's no record of Texas Tech jumping into the Colt McCoy recruiting pool. That cleared the deck for three other major college football programs in Texas—the University of Texas, Texas A&M, and the University of Houston—to ramp up their efforts in the spring of Colt's junior year. Duke, Stanford, and Kansas State said they wanted in, too.

Like the Bradfords in Oklahoma, the McCoys huddled up and decided to have Colt verbally commit to a college before his senior year of high school football. Now it was a matter of finding the right school.

In May 2004, at the end of Colt's junior year, he was running at the UIL (University Interscholastic League) State Track and Field Meet, held on the University of Texas campus in Austin. (Colt was a three-sport athlete at Jim Ned, playing basketball all four years and running the 110-meter hurdles and mile relay on the track team for three seasons.)

While Colt was in Austin, he and Brad visited with Long-horns coach Mack Brown, and they felt comfortable with him for several reasons. Like Sam, Colt had attended a col-lege football camp between his sophomore and junior year, and he "fell in love" with the University of Texas program after attending Mack Brown's summer camp. They also liked the offensive system the Longhorn coaches had installed.

It wasn't a difficult decision; Texas wanted him, the Mc-Coys liked Texas, so UT it would be.

"I kind of did this [committing to the Longhorns] to get it off my shoulders," Colt told Danny Reagan of the *Abilene Reporter-News*.

Brad said, "Ultimately, he decided he wanted to stay in state," which surprised no one who knew the McCoy family. "He really likes what's going on at Texas right now."

What made the decision an all-orange slam dunk was a bit of news that the McCoy family had known for a while. Jordan Shipley, Colt's close friend since their grade school days, had signed a letter of intent to play at the University of Texas back on National Signing Day a few months earlier. A grade ahead of Colt, he would be enrolling the following August.

The possibility of playing pass-and-catch with his best friend before 89,000 rabid fans at Darrell K. Royal-Texas Me-morial Stadium was too exciting for Colt to contemplate.

NOTHING TO SEE HERE

After Colt committed to Texas, major newspapers sent reporters to Tuscola to snoop around. In small towns, where everyone knew each other's business, surely there was a skeleton buried in Colt's closet.

None could dig up any dirt on Colt. *Nada.*

Elderly couples described how Colt waved to passing cars while he mowed lawns for spending money. Teachers doted on the youngster who pulled down straight-A report cards. Townspeople talked about how he picked up trash by the side of the road as part of the Don't Mess with Texas program. He also delivered dinners to shut-ins with Meals on Wheels, and a couple of times a week during the school year he tutored elementary school kids with their reading. When a tornado blew through town but didn't touch down, some said that Colt lassoed the twister and rode away on it.

At Jim Ned, Colt was a student council leader, office aide, 2004 Class Favorite, Most Outstanding Male Athlete, and Mr. Jim Ned High School. He was a member of the National Honor Society with a grade-point average of 98.2 on a 100-point scale.

Colt's senior year of football was very much like his junior year, but now he had a new target to throw to—his brother Chance, a sophomore. The brother-to-brother tandem connected on 67 completions for 1,000 yards and 15 touchdowns. One can only imagine the laughter and fun the McCoy family enjoyed around the dinner table that special season.

Jim Ned breezed into the state 2A playoffs undefeated, but Canadian High, the eventual state champion, upended the Indians 32–27. This time there were no tears. Colt's high school career was in the books: a 34–2 record, more than five miles of passing (9,344 yards), and 116 touchdown passes. He was the best passer in Texas 2A football history.

Just before Colt graduated in June 2005, Brad accepted the job as head football coach at Graham High in Graham, Texas. This was a 3A school, so Chance would see an upgrade in competition. Plus, Brad and Debra had their youngest son, Case, to think about. He was entering the seventh grade and playing quarterback in youth football.

The move didn't take the McCoys much farther from Austin, though. Tuscola was just over 200 miles from Austin (about four hours one way) while Graham was 240 miles (around four and a half hours) away.

The move's dividend was that Graham was just 100 miles west of the Dallas/Fort Worth Airport. When Colt played on the road, Brad and Debra wanted to be there.

The family wasn't about to miss Game Day.

ARRIVING IN AUSTIN

Colt had one good thing going for him when he stepped on the UT campus as a student in 2005: he was the only quarterback among the 15 incoming players the Longhorns signed that recruiting season.

What he didn't have going for him—at least not at first—was a body developed well enough to play football in the Big 12 Conference. At the start of training camp, Texas offensive coordinator Greg Davis looked at the new 170-pound recruit and said, "Gosh almighty, son, get into the weight room and talk to me later."

Colt didn't fight him. He knew he looked like a "skinned

squirrel"—his own words—compared with the behemoths who play NCAA Division 1 football. So Colt did three things during his 2005 redshirt season to prepare himself for the college level:

1. added 10 to 15 pounds of muscle in the weight room

2. quarterbacked the scout team against the first-team and second-team defense

3. shadowed star junior quarterback Vince Young from the practice field to team meetings to film room

Even though Colt knew he wasn't going to play his first year at Texas, he still suited up for games and was listed as third quarterback—behind Young and senior Matt Nordgren—on the Longhorn depth chart. Coach Mack Brown was careful to preserve the extra year of eligibility for Colt, however, and didn't play him a single down during the 2005 season.

Besides, the jump from 2A high school football to a major college program like Texas called for taking things slow and easy. There was no hurry to rush Colt along; Vince Young had two more years of Texas football eligibility ahead of him.

But after Young posted a monster season in 2005, including his clutch dash to the end zone at the BCS National Championship Game, NFL scouts started drooling. With tens of millions of dollars being waved in his face, Young opted to leave early for professional football.

Texas offensive coordinator Greg Davis remembers Colt approaching him the day after Young announced he was making himself available for the NFL draft. "Colt said, 'Coach, I want to be the best quarterback that you've ever had.' At the time, Colt was about 184 pounds, and Vince Young was a massive man [6 feet, 5 inches tall and 223 pounds]. I'm thinking, *Vince is leaving and I've got Pee Wee Herman sitting across the desk from me, and he's telling me that he's going to be the best quarterback there's ever been around here.*"

As the departure of Rhett Bomar from Oklahoma paved the way for Sam Bradford, the early exit of Vince Young for the NFL created a nice opening for Colt.

And he was going to make the most of the opportunity.

A QUARTERBACK CONTROVERSY?

Colt found out in spring practice that the Longhorn upperclassmen weren't exactly welcoming him to their huddle with open arms. There were four offensive linemen on the team who would be fourth- or fifth-year seniors the following fall—and three would go on to play in the NFL. Colt said, "They were like, 'I'm not listening to you, dude. You're a freshman.' "

The Texas coaches caught the vibe, so Davis concocted a no-huddle offense with the idea that Colt, who said he could "barely spit out" plays because of nerves, couldn't be mocked by his senior linemen since there was no huddle before each play.

Colt was still a baby-faced, wide-eyed, and fairly scrawny redshirt freshman coming into summer training camp. But winning over the Neanderthals with stubble beards was the least of Colt's worries; he was in a quarterback competition with someone even *younger* than he was—Jevan Snead, a blue-chip recruit from Stephenville, Texas, who had verbally committed to the University of Florida but backed out when the Gators landed a recruit named Tim Tebow.

There was also the lingering hangover from Vince Young's departure. Coach Mack Brown said, "I thought Vince would come back, very honestly. I might have been the only one in America that did."

But Young was off to the Tennessee Titans, and Coach Brown and his staff needed to retool the Longhorn offense in a hurry. Texas was the national champion defending a 20-game winning streak, so even though the cupboard was being restocked, expectations of the fans and media for a tasty 2006 season remained high. *Sports Illustrated* ranked Texas as the No. 3 team in the country in its College Football Preview issue.

As was the case in Norman with Sam Bradford, the Texas quarterback competition would be settled in team scrimmages played under real game conditions: striped referees, a game clock, and every play being filmed for later review. Colt, the coaches and the media agreed, looked like the first-teamer all the way. His presence on the field, as well as his decision making and poised throws, proved he was ready. Colt's redshirt season had given him an extra year of college experience over Jevan Snead. There would be no quarterback controversy at Texas in 2006—unlike the one earlier in the decade featuring Major Applewhite and Chris Simms.

When Colt won the job, the sportswriters on the Longhorns beat made "Colt .45" outlaw puns or referred to him as the "the Real McCoy," a reference to Joseph McCoy, a nineteenth-century cattle baron who made good on his pledge to ship a number of Longhorn cattle from Texas to Kansas.

But still, everyone wondered if Colt could handle the pressure and perform well once the 2006 season started.

A HERO TO THE RESCUE

After his first season of spring practice in 2006, Colt drove home for Memorial Day weekend. A little less than a year earlier, his parents had moved from Tuscola to Graham, an oil town of 8,700, when Brad took the head coaching job at Graham High School. The family purchased a home on Timber Ridge Lake, a sliver of water a mile and a half long and 300 or 400 yards across. No motor boats or electric boats were allowed on the private lake, but residents could use paddle boats to get to their favorite fishing holes.

Around 9 P.M. on Memorial Day, Colt and Brad stepped outside the back of their home. It was completely dark outside—no moon—and they had fished all day long. Then they heard it: a cry of desperation traveling across the waters.

"This is Patina. Ken and I are on the dock. He's having a grand mal seizure. Call 911," the shaky voice called out in the distance.

Several minutes earlier, Patina Herrington, who lived across the lake from the McCoys, had heard Annabelle, a chocolate Labrador who lived next door, scratching on her glass doors. She grabbed a flashlight and asked, "Annabelle, what's going on?"

The excited dog ran toward the lake and quickly returned to Patina, then repeated the nervous behavior. Annabelle had never acted like this before. Patina knew something was wrong.

Then Patina remembered: Ken, her 60-year-old husband, had gone to the dock to check something out.

The Herringtons' house was perched above the lake. To reach the water, Patina followed a series of steps cut through big boulders. With Annabelle leading the way, Patina rushed to the dock with her heart in her throat. She had reason to worry; her husband had suffered numerous seizures over the years and had undergone three brain surgeries that contributed to aphasia, a speech disorder.

When Patina reached the dock, her husband was thrashing about. He was in the midst of a grand mal seizure—violent muscle contractions accompanied by a loss of consciousness.

Patina rushed to Ken's side, cradled him in her arms, and attempted to stop him from biting his tongue. As he continued to thrash about, she realized they were both in a horrible fix. The Herringtons didn't own a cell phone, and she couldn't leave him on the dock to run back to the house to call 911. If she did, Ken could twist and twitch himself into the lake and drown. But if she couldn't call 911, Ken was doomed.

"Somehow, I knew everything was going to be okay," Patina said. "I wasn't alone because God was with me."

She screamed into the darkness for help, hoping someone would hear her.

Two sets of neighbors heard her desperate plea: Sandra Boedeker, who lived directly across the lake, four doors from the McCoys, and Brad and Colt. Sandra called 911 and asked the dispatcher to send an ambulance to the Herrington residence immediately.

The McCoys didn't hesitate. Father and son sprinted for the dock, jumped into the lake, and swam toward the Herrington home like it was a 400-meter Olympic freestyle final. Neither took their shirts or shoes off before hitting the water.

Halfway across the lake, Colt, who was outpacing his father, lost both sneakers because he was kicking so furiously. He arrived first and hauled himself onto the dock. In the distance, a siren could be heard in the still night.

"How can I help?" Colt asked as he came alongside Mrs. Herrington.

"My husband's not good," she replied. "If the EMTs don't get here soon—"

"You stay here with him. I'll go tell them where we are."

Patina watched as a soaking wet and barefoot Colt raced up the boulder wall to the house. He couldn't see the path her husband had cut into the stones, but he showed no concern for his own well-being as he scampered up the boulders in bare feet. Then he raced to Timber Ridge Road so he could flag down the EMTs. The distance from dock to the street was probably 200 yards.

Colt guided the EMTs back to the dock and helped them lower a gurney, then climbed down the boulders again and assisted them as they lifted a now-stabilized Ken into the stretcher. Colt held the IV and escorted the EMTs back to their emergency vehicle every step of the way.

"Thank goodness Colt was in *good* shape," Patina said. "Bless his heart. Ken had consecutive grand mal seizures, and doctors told us that if Colt had arrived five minutes later, my husband probably wouldn't have made it. His body was worn out."

The Herringtons became even bigger fans of Colt after his Good Samaritan gesture. "Ken graduated from UT in 1968, and I went there but never graduated, so we love the Longhorns. We never try to see Colt after a game, though. We would never intrude in that way. He gets mobbed by everybody. We prefer to say hi and hello when he's here in Graham. He and his dad have come over to the house a few times to check up on Ken, which is always appreciated."

Do they swim over?

"No," Patina laughed. "They drive a car. There's one more story. About six months after the incident, one of Colt's sneakers washed up on shore. It was a Nike. When I gave the shoe back to Colt, he laughed.

"We never found the other sneaker, though."

Colt had before him the unenviable task of following a legend—Vince Young—and he wasn't given much time to get settled in. Circled on the calendar was a home date with No. 1-ranked Ohio State on the second weekend of the season—an early showdown that would set the course of Longhorns' season. A loss would probably scuttle any hopes Texas had of repeating as national champions.

The Longhorns opened the season by dismantling North Texas, so the matchup with Ohio State was billed as another Big, Big Game between the top two teams in the country.

Texas Senator Kay Bailey Hutchison and Ohio Senator Mike DeWine placed a friendly wager on the outcome: Hutchison bet a couple of half-gallons of Blue Bell Ice Cream and DeWine staked some of his wife's homemade chocolate-covered peanut butter Buckeye candies.

Senator Hutchison had to find some dry ice for shipping because Texas lost decisively, 24–7. The loss was pinned on the Longhorn defensive secondary, which allowed Ohio State's Troy Smith to throw for 269 yards and two touchdowns. When Texas had the ball, the coaching staff kept Colt on a short leash: lots of screen passes and underneath routes. It wasn't his fault that receiver Billy Pittman fumbled on the Texas 2-yard line and an Ohio State player picked up the ball and ran it back to midfield, silencing the record crowd of 89,422—the most to ever watch a football game in the state of Texas. The lost fumble completely turned around the momentum.

In a strange way, the loss to Ohio State was freeing for Texas. During the rest of the 2006 season, the Longhorns weren't playing to protect a No. 1 ranking or a 21-game winning streak. Instead, they ran out on the field each week to have fun . . . and to beat the opposing team into sawdust. What followed was another winning streak—eight games this time—including a Red River Rivalry victory over Oklahoma.

Why the surge? Offensive coordinator Greg Davis opened up the Texas playbook, and Colt responded by playing so spectacularly that writers began touting the redshirt freshman as a possible Heisman Trophy candidate. He managed the offense well, made great throws, picked up blitzes, and took his share of shots. He showed tremendous poise in four come-from-behind victories: over Oklahoma (in Dallas), Baylor (down 10–0 at home), Nebraska (in blowing snow in Lincoln), and Texas Tech (in Lubbock, after falling behind 21–0 in the first quarter).

The QB was clutch. For two months, Colt played way beyond anyone's expectations.

The 2006 season ended on a down note, however. A 45–42 loss to Kansas State was one that got away, and Colt had to leave late in the game with a "stinger" injury to his neck. The following week, Texas A&M upset Texas 12–7 in the Big 12 Conference Title game.

The Longhorns, however, finished with a victory over Iowa in the Alamo Bowl. The win gave the 'Horns a 10–3 season and kept intact a six-year streak of winning at least 10 games. Colt threw for 29 touchdowns, tying the NCAA single-season record for TD passes by a freshman, and his 161.8 passer rating (a formula for evaluating a quarterback based on his completion percentage, passing yardage, touchdown passes, and interceptions) ranked him eighth nationally.

Better yet, Burnt Orange fans were talking more about Colt and his future instead of lamenting what-could-have-been had Vince Young stuck around for his senior season.

One other thing happened after the 2006 season: with Colt entrenched as the starting quarterback in Austin, Jevan Snead "unhooked 'em Horns" and transferred to Ole Miss—the University of Mississippi.

SWIMMING UPHILL

Colt was on a lot of watch lists after his amazing freshman season, but the pressure never lets up when you're the quarterback of the University of Texas. If Colt's 2007 season could be summed up with one word, it would be this: adversity.

The Longhorn offensive line was in disarray after the graduation of four starters from the 2006 team. Six players were disciplined for alleged infractions, and another was suspended for NCAA rules violations. One of Colt's top receivers, Limas Sweed, sat out most of the season with a wrist injury. The running game was nonexistent for the first half of the season. To add a final cup of flour, running backs coach Ken Rucker announced during summer training camp that he had been diagnosed with prostate cancer and would take a leave of absence to undergo surgery.

Add it all up, and you have a recipe for one of Texas' most tumultuous seasons.

The first month started innocently enough, although a season-opening victory over Arkansas State was too close for comfort. Still, the Longhorns were ranked No. 7 going into a home tilt against Kansas State, but the Wildcat defense, using a relentless pass rush, pounded Colt into his worst game as a

Texas quarterback, including four interceptions. KSU defensive end Ian Campbell ran the first pick back 41 yards for a touchdown, and Kansas State was on its way to a 41–21 beatdown. It was Mack Brown's worst home defeat in 10 years as the UT coach.

Colt had to run for his life most of the afternoon; the statistician recorded 13 "hurries" and seven tipped passes. A jarring hit just before halftime left Colt feeling woozy, and although he returned in the second half, he didn't finish the game. By game's end, he was vomiting on the sidelines, and Texas team officials later stated Colt had suffered a "mild concussion."

The following week, Colt got his first up-close look at Sam Bradford in the Red River Rivalry game. Oklahoma was ranked higher and favored, but the game was tied 21–21 early in the fourth quarter when the Sooners started a drive on their own six-yard line. All Colt could do was watch Sam make timely third-and-three and third-and-five passes to keep the winning drive alive. The Sooners won 28–21.

Texas fans thought the world had come to an end, but the Longhorns came back to win four straight games. A nationally televised day-after-Thanksgiving loss to Texas A&M, however, stuck in the craws of Longhorn fans. How could the Aggies—a .500 team at the time—beat mighty Texas 38–20?

"It's really hard," Texas defensive back Brandon Foster said. "You never enjoy losing, but losing to the Aggies is even worse."

Colt's two fumbles and an interception didn't help matters against Texas A&M, but that wasn't the only game in which he and the Longhorn offense struggled. His 18 interceptions in 2007 often thwarted the Longhorn offense. In Colt's defense, though, 10 of the picks came off tipped or deflected passes.

Texas ended the season on a bright note, taking a lopsided 52–34 Holiday Bowl victory against Arizona State. Colt won Offensive MVP honors despite fumbling four times. A second straight 10–3 season, though, didn't satisfy many Longhorn fans, players, or coaches. They wondered if UT could get over the hump and win 11, 12, or even 13 games in 2008.

If so, Colt would have to raise his quarterbacking to the elite level.

AN OUT-OF-COUNTRY EXPERIENCE

In March 2008, during spring break, Colt did something that helped him forget the uneven 2007 season and the fact that he was a Texas quarterback playing under the media microscope: he traveled to Peru on a missions trip organized by the Texas chapter of the Fellowship of Christian Athletes and T Bar M, a Texas organization that runs Christian youth sports camps.

Colt had plugged into the FCA chapter on the University of Texas campus from the get-go, but that was as natural to him as going to church on Sunday mornings. He had been involved with FCA Huddles since he was in middle school, when at the age of 14 he made a firm commitment to the Lord. His grandfather, Burl McCoy, had the honor of baptizing his grandson at his ranch south of Abilene.

Colt matured spiritually through high school, just as he was maturing into his leadership role on the football field.

Do your best and be a leader.

When it came to spiritual leadership, Colt led by example during his five years at the University of Texas. It was a rare week when he and Jordan Shipley missed a service at Westover Hills Church of Christ in Austin. Much of what Colt did on the "ministry" side while he was at Texas didn't get talked about a whole lot, which was fine with him.

He wasn't a bystander at FCA Huddle meetings on the UT campus, though. He loved hearing the speakers and hanging out with his buddies, including Jordan, kicker Hunter Lawrence, and center Chris Hall, who was a PK—a pastor's kid. There were a ton of Christians playing football, as well as other sports, for the University of Texas.

THE REAL DEAL

During Colt's senior year at Texas, he met on Thursday evenings with some teammates who were involved with FCA. The players gathered together at one of their homes for fellowship, study, and accountability.

They focused on trust, beginning with Jeremiah 17:7 ("But blessed is the man who trusts in the LORD, whose confidence is in him") and Jeremiah 29:11 (" 'For I know the plans I have for you,' declares the LORD, 'plans to prosper you and not to harm you, plans to give you hope and a future' ").The players made an agreement that when they stepped on the field, having given their lives to Christ, they had nothing to gain, nothing to lose, and nothing to prove (Colossians 3:1).

Reagan Lambert, who has been working with and discipling athletes at the University of Texas for 20 years, said Colt is the real deal. "He has a great sense of humor, and he's humble and fun to be around," Lambert said.

On many Fridays before home games, Colt joined a pas-
sel of Texas players who visited Dell Children's Medical Center in Austin, including the cancer ward. He also volunteered
for The Rise School of Austin (a school that assists children
with disabilities), Children's Miracle Network Telethon, the
Make-a-Wish Foundation, Caritas of Austin (which provides
food for the homeless), and the Boys and Girls Club.

So it wasn't a stretch for Colt to say yes when he was asked
if he wanted to go to Peru with a missions team over the 2008
spring break. The idea intrigued him, especially because he
had heard his grandparents, Burl and Jan McCoy, talk about
the medical missions trips they had taken to Africa.

But first, he had to clear things with Coach Brown and
offensive coordinator Greg Davis. They gave their blessing,
no doubt understanding the indelible impression a 10-day
missions trip to South America would make on any college
student athlete.

A long flight to the Peruvian capital of Lima was followed
by a shorter flight to Iquitos, a city of nearly 400,000 in the
Amazon rain forest that is considered the largest city in the
world that cannot be reached by road. The team was bused
into the jungle and the Amazon River basin, where they
jumped on motorboats for transportation to tiny villages
along the river. The natives lived in huts with dirt floors—
or muddy floors during the rainy season. With muggy 85
percent humidity and 100-degree heat, this wasn't the Four
Seasons.

The trip to the Peruvian rain forest was a wonderful,
life-changing, humbling experience for Colt on many levels.
First of all, the local kids had no idea who he was or what

an "American football" player did—they played *futbol*, but it wasn't the same sport—so he wasn't pestered for autographs or treated any differently than the others on the trip. "Nobody had any concept of what we do in the United States," Colt said. "I'm just another guy. Nobody knows who you are. You can just be yourself for a week."

Colt's "job" was to play with the kids, distribute clothes and other necessities, and share the gospel. Every meal came with a heaping bowl of rice, but Colt detested rice. By the time he returned to Austin, he had lost 15 pounds, which Greg Davis surely noticed.

Back to the weight room.

The biggest thing Colt learned from his Peru experience was that as a young man living in America, he had nothing to complain about. The grinding poverty overwhelmed him, but the Peruvian kids' attitude of happiness amazed him. He realized he had been like most Americans: having no clue of how people outside our borders live and the conditions they survive under. He returned to Austin with a greater perspective on his circumstances and how much he had to be thankful for.

The Peruvian kids, of course, didn't know a *Yanqui* sports celebrity was in their midst. But when Colt returned to Iquitos a year later with the same missions team, the kids were excited at his return. It seems the translators had pooled their money to rent a motorcycle so one of them could ride to a neighboring village and check on the Internet to see how the 'Horns did throughout the 2008 season.

Traveling to Peru for two missions trips was just the tip of the iceberg of how Colt gave back while he was at the University of Texas. Following his peerless freshman year, the requests to speak before various high school and youth groups, as well as FCA gatherings, came by the bushel, as many as 10 a day.

At one time, Colt accepted so many invitations to share his faith and inspire others that Greg Davis called Colt's father and asked him if he could help persuade his son to slow things down a bit.

Fat chance.

Colt McCoy had never been one to run away from an incoming rush.

PLAYING FOR SOMETHING BIGGER THAN HIMSELF

Colt came back from Peru energized and eager to put his "sophomore slump"—that's what the media was calling the Longhorns' 10–3 season—behind him. "I hate that term," Colt said. "It's not a slump because I feel like I grew so much, I got better, understood the offenses, and gained a ton of experience that's going to help me this year."

The media was also calling the 2008 campaign a rebuilding season, but Coach Brown quelled that talk. There are no rebuilding years at Texas, he said.

The fact that Texas didn't lose in September or October was all Colt. The inexperience on the Longhorn interior line meant he had to absorb too many late hits or scramble for yards. Time after time, though, Colt made plays. His nimble feet allowed him to escape blitzes or turn busted plays into big gains. *Sports Illustrated*'s college beat columnist wrote, "McCoy escapes from seemingly impossible situations so often, The Watch wonders if his real surname isn't actually MacGyver."

The Red River Rivalry game of 2008 was certainly worthy of a prime-time show. The matchup pitted the undefeated and No. 5-ranked Longhorns against the top team in the country—Sam Bradford-led Oklahoma. The eyes of sporting America were on the Cotton Bowl, and rightly so.

Oklahoma took an early lead, but a Jordan Shipley 96-yard kickoff return for a touchdown in the second quarter cut into a 14–3 deficit and sparked the Longhorns. Then Colt tossed his childhood friend a short touchdown pass in the third quarter to tighten the score, 28–27, with Texas still behind. Jordan's crucial third-and-eight reception in the fourth quarter led to Texas' first lead, 38–35, and the 'Horns won going away, 45–35.

Now the Longhorns were the top dog, to mix metaphors, as well as the No. 1 team in the country.

Some rebuilding year.

An important road contest—another Big Game, as the ESPN talking heads would say—loomed in Lubbock, the home of Texas Tech. Coach Mike Leach had the sixth-ranked Red Raiders in top form, and emotions ran high on the home-field side of the ball. Texas Tech leaped to a 19–0 lead, and, on a Saturday night in Lubbock, coming back from a nearly three-touchdown deficit was a tall order.

But Colt led a stunning rally, and with a little more than a minute to go, a grinding Longhorn drive resulted in a 33–32 Texas lead.

This might have been one of Colts' greatest wins, but the Longhorn defense still had to make a final stop. On the game's final play—one that would seemingly be replayed eight million times on ESPN—Tech quarterback Graham Harrell zipped a pass to receiver Michael Crabtree, who caught the ball near the sideline and somehow miraculously broke away from two Longhorn defenders and kept his balance as he tip-toed down the sideline without falling out of bounds. Crabtree stepped into the end zone with one second to play, and Texas lost a heartbreaker, 39–33.

DEDICATING A SEASON TO A FALLEN HERO

When Colt suited up during the 2008 season, he adopted a ritual: reaching into his locker for a silver crucifix on a chain and putting it around his neck. He only wore the simple cross during games.

The crucifix belonged to his cousin, Grant Hinds, who was several years older than Colt. As kids, they hunted, fished, and rode four-wheelers together. Then Grant joined the Marines and went off to war. He returned from three tours of duty in Iraq and Afghanistan in one piece physically, but he battled post-traumatic stress disorder, nightmares, and depression. The member of a tank battalion, Grant had witnessed death and destruction.

Following his discharge, Grant enrolled at Kennesaw State University in Georgia, where he suffered a brain hemorrhage and died following a car accident. He was only 25 years old.

Colt dedicated his 2008 season to the cousin who had died five months earlier. "Every game I say, 'This is for Grant.' I want to play with the same heart and attitude he had with all the courage it took to fight for us," Colt said.

Colt, who didn't dedicate any other of his seasons to anyone, wore Grant's crucifix under his shoulder pads as a reminder that he was playing for someone else—the memory of a close cousin.

The bitter loss dropped Texas to No. 4 in the country, but that would be the Longhorns' only blemish of the 2008 campaign. Colt's great performances vaulted him into the Heisman race, and he traveled with his parents to New York City, where he met Sam Bradford and Tim Tebow in person.

Although he didn't win the Heisman—he finished second—Colt's 2008 season meant that when the topic of college football's top quarterbacks came up, you couldn't talk about Sam Bradford or Tim Tebow without also mentioning Colt McCoy's name.

It seemed the three of them were joined at the hips.

THE FINAL CAMPAIGN

At least the media didn't ask Mack Brown the following question when the University of Texas football team broke training camp: *Coach, your team was 12–1 in 2008 and finished as only the No. 3 team in the country. Would you call this a rebuilding year?*

That's Longhorn football for you. But everything is bigger in Texas, right? You only had to gaze at the recent opening of the palatial Cowboys Stadium to get a sense of how big—and important—football is to Texas. NFL owner Jerry Jones had spent $1.2 billion to construct the largest domed stadium in the world, including the world's largest high-definition video screen, which hung above the field from the 20-yard line to the 20-yard line.

Do you watch the game or watch the game on those huge TV screens above your seat?

The 2009 season was it for fifth-year senior quarterback Colt McCoy. Tim Tebow had already grasped two NCAA team championships, and Sam Bradford had played in the BCS National Championship Game the previous January, losing to the Tebow-led Florida Gators. Now it was Colt's turn.

Heading into the season, most everyone was saying it would be Florida, Oklahoma, or Texas fighting it out at the Rose Bowl in January. "The Top Three Quarterbacks on the Top Three Teams," declared a *SportingNews* headline.

Would Colt get his chance to win a national championship?

For that to happen, the Longhorns couldn't afford to lose. All fall, the Texas football team played like they knew the score. The Longhorns earned revenge against Texas Tech in the third game of the season, beating the Red Raiders 34–24, and they were 7–0 before the Red River Rivalry game against Oklahoma.

Sam Bradford was trying to come back from a shoulder injury and wasn't thought to be 100 percent for the game against the Longhorns. When Texas cornerback Aaron Williams hit Sam on a blitz early in the game and ended his season, it seemed inconceivable that Oklahoma could weather the loss of their Heisman Trophy-winning quarterback. The Texas offense, however, couldn't find its rhythm. The Oklahoma defense confused Colt with five blitzes he'd never seen before. At halftime, Texas trailed 6–3 and Colt was only 7-of-16 passing.

The Longhorns eked out a 16–13 lead in the fourth quarter, and Texas had the ball when disaster nearly struck. Colt threw an interception, and just when it appeared his worst nightmare would happen before his eyes—a pick leading to a game-winning touchdown against his team's greatest rival—Colt scrambled and made the game-saving tackle. The defense then did its job and held, and Colt ground out the last 3:31, punctuated by an uncharacteristic fist pump toward the Burnt Orange end of the Cotton Bowl just before he took a knee on the final play of the game.

"Good teams find a way to win," said Coach Brown after the game.

That time-honored football truism summed up the 2009 season. The Longhorns didn't overwhelm many teams, and they never looked unbeatable, but they were never outscored.

The award for Biggest Squeaker of the Year would probably go to Texas following the Big 12 Championship game against No. 21-ranked Nebraska. A tough one the entire way: Colt was sacked nine times and threw three interceptions. Four and a half of those sacks came from Ndamukong Suh, the 6-foot, 5-inch, 305-pound defensive tackle who on one play whirlybirded Colt at least seven yards through the air.

After Nebraska had taken a 12–10 lead with 1:44 to play, an out-of-bounds kickoff put the Longhorns on their own 40-yard line. On the first play of the Texas drive, Colt found his favorite receiver, Jordan Shipley, for 19 yards; a horse-collar tackle added 15 more yards, and Texas was within field goal range on the Huskers' 26-yard line. (In case you're wondering why Jordan was still playing, since he was a grade ahead of Colt, the NCAA had granted him a sixth season of eligibility because he missed the entire 2004 and 2005 seasons due to knee and hamstring injuries.)

Seven seconds to go. Time for a quick play to get a little

closer. Then Colt nearly made a mistake that could have haunted him for years. He rolled to his right, a bit casually, and threw the ball out of bounds—and the clock read 00:00! Nebraska players swarmed the field in jubilation, believing they had won, but the play was reviewed in the replay booth. A trip to the national title game hung in the balance for Texas. After a long wait, the officials decided there was enough "time" left after Colt had thrown the ball out of bounds to put one second back on the clock.

And enough time to run one more play. Hunter Lawrence nailed a 46-yard field goal, and this time it was the Texas players who flung their helmets in the air and rushed the field to celebrate an unlikely victory and an undefeated 12–0 season.

The rifle-armed Colt McCoy had dodged a bullet.

A day later, Colt and the Texas team learned they had a date in Pasadena with the Alabama Crimson Tide for the BCS National Championship Game.

"It would mean a lot [to win against Alabama]," Colt said afterward. "I think it would put an end to four great years. That's what you fight for every year."

ROSE BOWL POSTSCRIPT

After suffering the shoulder injury while playing his last game in a Texas uniform, Colt flew home to decompress and hang out with his girlfriend, Rachel Glandorf.

Colt and Rachel met while she interned at KEYE Channel 42, Austin's CBS affiliate, when she covered the team as an on-camera reporter. Rachel attended Baylor University, 90 miles north of Austin, where she ran hurdles on the Bear track team. She was nine months younger than Colt.

Rachel had been sitting next to Colt's parents at Texas games throughout the 2009 season. Colt watchers speculated on where this relationship was heading.

When ESPN's Rick Reilly wrote in October 2009 that Rachel was "hotter than shrimp vindaloo," she hit the No. 1 spot in Google Trends. (Shrimp vindaloo, in case you're wondering, is a spicy Indian dish.)

Four days after the BCS Championship Game, Colt escorted Rachel to an empty Texas Memorial Stadium and walked her to the 50-yard line, smack dab in the middle of the field. He then pointed to the stadium's giant high-def scoreboard screen, which said in big, bold letters:

Rachel,

I love you!

Will you marry me?

Colt

When she turned around, Colt was bent down on one knee in the middle of the orange Longhorn logo, holding a small jewelry box that contained an engagement ring.

If and when Colt and Rachel have any children, their quarterback-playing sons won't have to worry about reaching optimal NFL height.

That's because the statuesque Rachel stands six feet tall.

3

TIM TEBOW:
THE CHOSEN ONE

Maybe you jumped ahead to this chapter because you love Tim Tebow.

Maybe you're thinking about skipping this chapter because you can't *stand* Tim Tebow.

Or maybe you're wondering why everyone is making such a big deal out of the Incredible Hulk in eye black.

In the pantheon of quarterbacks, college and pro, Tim Tebow is a rock star. He's the most talked-about football player in America and the most discussed, dissected, and debated athlete on ESPN, the arbiter of what's important in the sports world. When he's in public, he's a compelling figure who draws stares from bystanders, screams from fans, and clicks from cell phone cameras. He's been called the NFL version of a total solar eclipse, blotting out nearly every other name or topic in the football world.

His smile melts hearts. His demeanor is humble and

earnest. His attitude is respectful to elders and authority fig-
ures (like coaches), and his faith moves mountains. His work
ethic is off the charts. He's so good-natured and likeable that
you want to bottle him up and take him home to the family.

Tebowmania has broken out of the Southeast and is
sweeping the Rockies, home of the NFL's Denver Broncos.
Can the rest of the country be far behind?

Admit it—you can't keep your eyes off him. The camera
loves Tim Tebow. His emotions on the field run the gamut:
full-throated exhortations to his teammates, fist pumps and
helmet taps after big plays and touchdowns, broad smiles
and gracious interviews after victories, even emotional tears
in defeat.

If football was show business (and, in many ways, it's
hard to separate one from another), then Tim's charisma and
poise—that special "it"—defines his uniqueness, fortitude,
determination, and belief in himself. He has an amazing
presence on and off the field as well as a wonderful allitera-
tive roll to his name.

Tim Tebow is loved, hated, idolized, cheered, and booed
because his outsized personality broke the mold for the quarterback position during his four-year career at the University
of Florida. Once he plants his feet under or behind the center,
he plays QB like it's his personal fiefdom. He's as relentless
as Attila the Hun, as unstoppable as a Mack truck plowing
through a roadblock.

Now he's taking his win-at-all-costs game to the NFL
and the Denver Broncos. His agent, Jimmy Sexton, predicts
Tim will become the most marketable athlete in history. The
Davie-Brown Index, an independent marketing research firm

popular with brand marketers, found Tim to be more appealing and more of a trendsetter than three of the NFL's top quarterbacks: Tom Brady of the New England Patriots, Tony Romo of the Dallas Cowboys, and Brett Favre of the Minnesota Vikings—and that was *before* the 2010 NFL draft.

"Nobody seems to have popped out quite like Tebow," said Darin David, account director for The Marketing Arm agency.

Nike signed Tim to a shoe and apparel deal. EA Sports pasted a Gator-clad Tim on the cover of *NCAA Football 11*, which means you'll see his face and eye black plastered on the front window of every video game store in the country.

Expect more companies to launch Tim Tebow campaigns to coincide with his rookie season. Whether he's the starting quarterback for the Broncos, or he's being used in short-yardage "packages," or he's holding a clipboard with a clean jersey, you'll be hearing a lot about this special athlete.

IN THE BEGINNING

Timothy Richard Tebow was born August 14, 1987, in the Philippines.

In a manger.

Because his parents were told there was no room at the inn.

The part about Tim being born in the Philippines is true, but we're just having fun with his "nativity story." But this is the sort of mythmaking that happens when they start calling you "The Chosen One"—in high school.

Tim was born in Makati City, which is part of metro Manila, because his parents, Bob and Pam Tebow, were living in the Philippines as missionaries at the time. Bob and Pam met at the University of Florida in 1967, when Bob was a sophomore and Pam was a freshman. Unlike Kent Bradford and Brad McCoy, the fathers of the other two QBs, Bob Tebow wasn't on a college campus to play football, but he did see himself as an impact player. Even back then, Bob already knew his life's goal, and that was to share the message of Jesus Christ with others.

That was certainly a different goal than the one set forth by his father, whom Bob described as a workaholic who moved the family from Alabama to California to Florida as he developed a business in sales and finance. "Growing up, I knew my goal was to get a job and make a million dollars," Bob said.

That desire evaporated during a high school ski trip organized by Young Life, a ministry that reaches out to adolescents. The slopes were bare from warm weather that winter, which kept the Young Life group indoors for presentations and lectures. There, Bob heard the gospel message and became a Christian, a choice that would shape the rest of his life.

When Bob started attending the University of Florida, he and a close friend, Ander Crenshaw (who in 2001 began a career as a member of the U.S. House of Representatives, representing Florida's 4th congressional district) started a Campus Crusade for Christ chapter on the Gainesville campus.

Bob first met Pam when he was publicizing a Campus Crusade event. She was the daughter of a U.S. Army colonel who moved frequently when her father was assigned new postings, many beyond U.S. borders. She settled in Tampa during her high school years.

Bob and Pam became friends, and their first date came a year after they met, when Bob invited Pam to join him at . . . a football game between the University of Florida and the University of Georgia—a rivalry game played each year at a neutral site: Jacksonville. The Gators won, which just might have been a sign of good things to come.

Their love blossomed, and they graduated together from the University of Florida in 1971—he with a degree in health and human performance, and she with a degree from the College of Journalism and Communications. They married that summer and moved to Portland, Oregon, where Bob enrolled at Western Seminary to earn master's degrees in divinity and theology.

The extra schooling took five years. When Bob was finished, he and Pam moved back to Florida, where he became the area representative for the Fellowship of Christian Athletes (FCA) in the northeastern part of the state. Even though Bob had to raise his own support, he and Pam felt financially secure enough to start a family. After their first child, Christy, arrived in 1976, the parents spaced out Katie, Robby, Peter, and the family caboose—Tim—over the next 11 years.

Beginning in 1976, the Tebows started making major moves every three years. After a three-year stint with the FCA (1976–1979), Bob moved into church ministry at Southside Baptist Church in Jacksonville, where he was the associate pastor for three years until 1982. Then, for the next three years, he served as the pastor of Cornerstone Community Church, also in Jacksonville.

While at Cornerstone, Bob embarked on a life-changing

missionary trip to the Philippines. During the trip, he received what he believed was a call in his heart and a summons he could not deny: God was calling him to become a missionary in the Philippines.

Bob and Pam believed then, as they believe now, that God had been preparing their hearts for the mission field. And even though they had been praying He would open this door, think about how difficult this undertaking must have been for the family, especially Pam. She had three children, ages eight, six, and four, as well as an infant son, Peter, who was born in 1984. To pull up stakes in Jacksonville, where her husband was a respected pastor with a bright career ahead of him, and resettle the family in a third world country must have bordered upon the unreal for her.

They would be moving 12 time zones and almost exactly halfway around the world to Southeast Asia, a 19-hour plane trip that would take her far from the creature comforts of home. The logistics had to be daunting, the heartbreak of leaving behind friends and family gut-wrenching. They would have to sell most of their personal belongings. But to her credit, Pam never blinked. Living abroad as a young girl had certainly prepared her for this time in their lives. Besides, she was convinced this was God's will for their lives, and she was fine with that.

Before their departure, Bob founded the Bob Tebow Evangelistic Association with five priorities in mind:

1. Train and employ Filipinos as full-time evangelists since the Philippine culture would naturally respond better to the gospel message when they heard it from fellow countrymen.

2. Plant churches throughout the Philippines, which is an archipelago made up of 7,107 islands and categorized broadly into three main geographical divisions: Luzon, Visayas, and Mindanao.

3. Host periodic conferences in several Asian countries to train even more pastors and local people how to talk to others in their country about their faith.

4. Organize summer mission trips to the Philippines for American young people.

5. Open an orphanage to care for the least of these.

The family settled outside Manila, the capital city of the Philippines, and the transition went as smoothly as they dared hoped for. Filipinos were being trained as pastors, and countless locals were embracing the Christian faith. The Tebow kids—who had yet to reach their teenage years—acclimated well. "It wasn't always easy, but it was a wonderful time for our family," Pam said. "We learned a lot—you always learn a lot when you [live in] a third world country."

A year after their arrival, Bob was out in the mountains in Mindanao. "I was showing a film and preaching that night," he told *Sports Illustrated*. "I was weeping over the millions of babies being [aborted] in America, and I prayed, 'God, if you give me a son, if you give me Timmy, I'll raise him to be a preacher.'"

The previous sentence is taken word for word from a *Sports Illustrated* article that ran in the summer of 2009. Did you notice the editorializing? Writer Austin Murphy and/or the SI editors inserted the word "aborted" in brackets to signify that the magazine was not using the original word Bob said, or, in this case, wrote because Bob Tebow was responding to questions that had been e-mailed to him.

So what do you think Bob originally typed? Since he is ardently pro-life, you have to figure that he tapped out this sentence on his computer screen:

I was weeping over the millions of babies being killed in America...

That's how strongly he—and Pam—felt about abortion, which stops a beating heart and ends the life of a growing human being. Their hearts wept at the carnage of 4,000 abortions that happen every day in the United States, or 1.5 million each year.

Sports Illustrated—and the Tebows would tell you the world feels the same way—didn't like the starkness or the reality of the word *killed*. So they chose to insert *aborted* instead. More clinical. Easier to brush off, sweep under the rug.

And then Pam got pregnant with Tim, and she and Bob suddenly had to confront their beliefs about the sanctity of life and the sovereignty of Almighty God.

A CHOICE

When Pam became pregnant with Tim, she was 37 years old, living 9,000 miles from home, the mother of four energetic children, and the wife of a missionary pastor.

The pregnancy was not unexpected. In fact, she and Bob very much desired to have a fifth child. They had been praying for Timmy by name—to this day, they still call him "Timmy" and not "Tim"—before she conceived. They wanted to name their son after the young church leader named Timothy, who was the recipient of a pair of letters from the apostle Paul that now appear in the New Testament.

Just before she became pregnant, however, Pam contracted amoebic dysentery, a disease caused by bacteria transmitted through contaminated drinking water. Dysentery is common in developing and tropical countries like the Philippines and is not to be taken lightly—between 40,000 and 100,000 people die worldwide each year of amoebic dysentery, and it was the leading cause of death in the Philippines. The disease causes inflammation of the intestines and bloody, severe diarrhea.

Pam fell into a coma, and she was treated aggressively with a series of strong antimicrobial drugs. As she came out of the coma and her condition stabilized, she continued to take the powerful medications.

Then the stick turned blue when she took a pregnancy test.

Pam recalled reading a label on her prescription warning that the antimicrobial drug could cause "severe birth defects." She immediately discontinued the treatment protocol, fearing that harm had already been done to the growing life inside her. When she told her doctor what had transpired, her worst fears were confirmed when she heard that her "fetus" had been irreversibly damaged. That being the case, the doctor recommended that she "discontinue" the pregnancy—in other words, have an abortion.

Actually, "They didn't recommend," Pam said. "They didn't really give me a choice. That was the only option they gave me."

To Pam and Bob, there was a lot more than a "fetus" growing inside her womb. This was a life, not a glob of tissue or a "product" of conception. Since the Tebows believed God was the author of life—and death—there was no doubt in their minds that they would trust Him in this perilous situation for her *and* for the unborn child.

Pam and Bob's decision was set in concrete, and their determination to see this pregnancy through didn't waver when Pam's doctor told her that her placenta had detached from the uterine wall—a dangerous development known as placental abruption. Pam was a 37-year-old, high-risk patient living in the Philippine countryside, and a severe condition like this one could have easily killed her. Once again, she was counseled to have an abortion—to save her own life. Certainly she would be justified in taking this measure. But Pam wouldn't consider it.

"We were determined to trust the Lord with the children He would give us," she said in an interview with Focus on the Family president Jim Daly. "And if God called me to give up my life, then He would take care of my family."

Bottom line: Pam Tebow wasn't just *willing* to risk her life for Timmy; she actually *chose* to risk her life so that her son might live.

At the seventh month of her crisis pregnancy, Pam traveled to Manila, where she remained on bed rest and received around-the-clock care from an American-trained physician. This was a touch-and-go pregnancy the entire way, and she and Bob prayed earnestly that God would give them the chance to raise the son they would name Timmy.

On her due date of August 14, Pam gave birth to Tim—and the family learned just how serious the placental abruption had been. "There was a great big clump of blood that came out where the placenta wasn't properly attached, basically for the whole nine months," Bob said in an interview with Focus on the Family. "He was a miracle baby."

He was also skinny and long—like the malnourished newborn he was. The Tebows asked friends and family to pray that their newborn son would grow up big and strong. "It was amazing that God spared him, but we knew God had His hand on his life," Bob said. "We all, through the years, have told Timmy that."

STILL GOING STRONG

These days, Bob Tebow continues to run the Bob Tebow Evangelistic Association (BTEA) with the goal of reaching as many of the 42,000 Philippine *barangays*, or villages, as possible with the gospel through 45 Filipino pastors the ministry supports. The BTEA evangelists have preached to more than 12 million people since 2002 and founded more than 8,000 churches, but nearly two-thirds of the *barangays* have no evangelical church. BTEA's plans call for increasing the staff of national evangelists to 60.

For more information, go online and visit the BTEA website at www.btea.org.

BACK IN THE USA

When Tim was three years old, the Tebow family decided to move back to Florida to be closer to home and family. After laying down a strong foundation and sending pastors out into the fields, Bob felt he could run the Bob Tebow Evangelistic Association from a distance while continuing to make periodic trips to the western Pacific Ocean. He could also organize short-term and summer mission trips to the Philippines better while living stateside.

The family moved back to the Jacksonville area and lived on a 44-acre farm tucked between the tranquil setting of Baldwin and the city of Jacksonville. When Tim was a kindergartner, he joined his four older sisters and brothers at a special school with a limited enrollment—the Tebow Homeschool.

Homeschooling was becoming better and better known to the general public in the 1980s, thanks to pioneers like Dr. Raymond Moore and his wife, Dorothy—educators who became vocal advocates for homeschooling, particularly among Christian families. Parents purchased curriculum packages and teaching aids geared to their children's ages. The Tebows were early adopters, beginning in 1982 with Christy.

Let's face it: homeschooling was a radical idea back then, and it's still looked upon in many circles as strange. How can children learn enough to get a good education or get into college if they don't receive instruction from trained teachers in public and private school classrooms?

The Tebows had some clear ideas on how they wanted to raise their children. They were wary of worldly influences intruding upon their five offspring—outside influences that would smack them the moment they stepped on the school bus. They were also greatly concerned about the moral and cultural values conveyed in the public school classroom setting.

So Bob and Pam sought a different approach. They wanted to inspire their children to love God, live excellently, be humble, and serve their fellow man. As hands-on parents who

would alone be responsible for their children's formal edu-
cations, they would be closely monitoring what came into
the home and would be intentional about the lessons their
children would learn.

"If I could get my kids to the age of 25 and they know God
and serve God and had character qualities that pleased God,
then I knew God would be happy and I would be happy," Bob
said. "The only way I could do that was to do it myself, commit to God that this is my job. Traditional academics had to
take a back seat to God's Word and character-building."

They started homeschooling Christy, Katie, Robby, and
Peter before the family moved to the Philippines. Pam taught
them the Three R's—reading, 'riting, and 'rithmetic—plus
other subjects as they got older. Everything their children
learned would be taught through the prism of the Bible and
with an emphasis on learning how to speak in public. Bob
and Pam wanted each of their children to feel comfortable
and confident in communicating their beliefs.

Many of the biblical lessons Bob and Pam taught their
children centered around themes of humility, honoring God,
and serving others. When each child was very young, Pam
chanted the words to one Bible truth in a sing-song voice. A
sample teaching:

A man who walks with wise men will be wise;
A man who walks with wise men will be wise;
A man who walks with wise men will be wise;
But the companion of fools will suffer harm.

Memorizing Bible verses, as well as life lessons, were
foundational to learning in the Tebow home. For instance,
Proverbs 27:2 (New King James Version) taught the children

not to brag on themselves:

Let another man praise you, and not your own mouth;
A stranger, and not your own lips.

Bob and Pam believed humility was one of the greatest measures of a person's character, so they constantly turned to the Bible and had their children memorize verses on humility, such as:

• Remember how the LORD your God led you all the way in the desert these forty years, to humble you and to test you in order to know what was in your heart, whether or not you would keep his commands (Deuteronomy 8:2).

• You save the humble, but your eyes are on the haughty to bring them low (2 Samuel 22:28).

• When pride comes, then comes disgrace, but with humility comes wisdom (Proverbs 11:2).

• The fear of the LORD teaches a man wisdom, and humility comes before honor (Proverbs 15:33).

• Humility and the fear of the LORD bring wealth and honor and life (Proverbs 22:4).

And if they wanted to see their children's eyes grow big, the parents read them the story of what happened to King Nebuchadnezzar after he took credit for what God had done. The king ended up on all fours munching grass like a cow— all because of pride.

When the children weren't memorizing Bible verses or doing their schoolwork, they learned discipline through chores like taking out the trash, vacuuming, making their beds, and washing dishes. That was just the beginning since there was always work to do on such a large property dotted with pines and grassy fields—work such as building fences, feeding the cows, and mowing the grass.

The parents turned a half-acre plot behind the house into a vegetable garden, and the children learned the value of stoop labor as they weeded with hoes and planted and cared for the vegetables that fed their family of seven year-round. They slaughtered and ate the cows they raised. Bucking fallen trees in the "back 40" was another way Bob instilled the value of physical labor in his sons.

Bob and Pam had a firm rule in the Tebow household: no complaining. That rule must have stuck because you can't call Tim Tebow a grumbler or a whiner today. That characteristic has shown itself on the few occasions when his team has lost a football game. While Tim deeply hates losing at anything he does, he's never been one to offer excuses.

NO GRAND PLAN

It's a great quip, a superb sound bite, and something Bob Tebow loves repeating. It goes like this:

"I asked God for a preacher, and He gave me a quarterback."

There was no grand plan in the Tebow family to raise a great athlete, let alone a star quarterback who would become an NFL first-round draft pick, and this makes Tim's story very much different than those of Sam Bradford and Colt McCoy.

Sam, as you read in his chapter, was the son of athletically minded parents who signed up their only child for just about every organized youth sport under the sun: football, basketball, baseball, and hockey. If he had a spare moment, he golfed with his grandfather and friends. The strategy worked:

Sam became a gifted athlete with incredible hand-eye coordination.

Colt was the son of a high school football coach, so he literally grew up at the knee of a father who loved the game. From the time he could walk, Colt hung around a football field, soaking it all in. Once he was old enough to play, he developed into an excellent quarterback, thanks in large part to the tutelage of his father.

Not so in the Tebow household, where sports were more low-key. Think about it: during their five years in the Philippines, there was no such thing as Little League or AYSO soccer. The kids played outside, ran around, and did things that little kids do, but there were no "travel teams" in the Philippines.

After the Tebow family returned to Florida, Christy played some tennis, and Katie was a runner. Tim's older brothers Robby and Peter got into youth baseball and football. The parents kept everything in perspective; they knew getting exercise was good for the body, but they didn't want their schedules revolving around sports. But the Tebows *were* into competition. "There was no mercy in our family," Bob said. "Katie, every once in a while, would show you mercy, but everyone else would cut your throat."

The Tebow family's competitive streak extended beyond sports. Board games like Monopoly quickly deteriorated into overheated emotions when a simple roll of the dice landed one of the Tebow kids on Boardwalk or Park Place teeming with red hotels. And woe to the Risk players when their territories were captured. When Bob taught each of his children how to play chess, the sparks would fly following a checkmate.

Bob told writer Guerry Smith he never let any of the children beat him at chess—and no one can topple his king to this day. The last time he challenged anyone to take him on, there were no takers. "It's pretty dog-eat-dog around here," he said. "They know the outcome."

With that thought in mind, Bob noticed something about Tim, even when his son was a five-year-old: he had a tremendous arm and impressive hand-eye coordination—as well as the Tebow competitive streak. Tim threw left-handed, but that was his natural side, so Bob didn't try to change him.

Tim could throw a football with excellent velocity for a pint-sized tyke, and when he had a bat in his hand, he could swing and hit the ball squarely. His parents thought he'd have fun playing T-ball, the pressureless entry point for youth baseball, so they signed him up. There's no live pitching in T-ball; each batter steps up to the plate and swings at a ball placed on a plastic tee. Once the player hits the ball into fair territory, he starts running.

Many five-year-olds are clueless about how baseball is played, and some prefer to lie down in the outfield and watch the clouds roll by. Not Tim, who played second base for the White Sox. If he had another gift besides pure athleticism, it was awareness of his surroundings. He would get perturbed when the other kids didn't know what was going on, as Guerry Smith described on Rivals.com:

> Some of his teammates were picking at the ground without even paying attention. *How is that possible?* he wondered. *There's a game going on. Focus*

on the game. He heard players say they were out there for the snow cone they would get when the game was over. Not Tebow. The competition was all that mattered at the moment. He heard his coach say, "You don't have to play to win. Just play to have fun," and he could not comprehend the mindset. *It's not fun if you don't win*, he said to himself. He was dumbfounded. He was also five years old.

Tim also played Pop Warner football. As one of the bigger kids on the team, he played tight end on offense and linebacker on defense. Then one day, when he was 11 years old, his coach, David Hess, watched him practice and said to himself, *This kid is such a talented athlete. He'd make a good quarterback.*

Hess asked Tim to get down on one knee and throw the ball as far as he could. The youngster heaved the ball 30 yards in the air. After that, Tim was lining up behind center. "Guess that's my claim to fame," Coach Hess said years later.

People who knew Tim during his Pop Warner days are still telling Tebow stories—like the time he lined up behind center on his team's 20-yard line and saw the tackles cheating a bit. Instead of taking the snap and tossing the ball to the tailback—the play called in the huddle—Tim ran a quarterback sneak . . . all the way into the end zone, 80 yards away.

When Tim wasn't flying past defenders, he was running over players who dared get in his way. Linebackers who searched for Tim in the open field to deliver a hit stopped searching after the first time they collided with him.

Then there was the tremendous arm strength his father

Sam Bradford rolls right, looking for a receiver in an October 2008 game won by the Sooners, 45–31.

Sam Bradford, the NFL's No. 1 draft overall draft pick of 2010, is greeted by league commissioner Roger Goodell at the Radio City Music Hall in New York City.

Ben Liebenberg, NFL.com

Sam Bradford looks to pass against Baylor in a 2009 game. Bradford threw for 389 yards to lead the Sooners to a 33–7 victory.
Sue Ogrocki, Associated Press

Shoulder wrapped, arm in sling, Sam Bradford watches the end of the Sooners' 2009 season opener against Brigham Young University. He would reinjure the shoulder later in the fall against Texas, ending his season.
Tony Gutierrez, Associated Press

Colt McCoy needed every second—literally—to lead the Longhorns to a come-from-behind 13–12 victory in the 2009 Big 12 championship game against Nebraska.

Amy Gutierrez, Associated Press

Texas quarterback Colt McCoy shakes hands with NFL quarterbacking legend Bart Starr after receiving the Johnny Unitas Golden Arm Award in December 2009.
Rob Carr, Associated Press

Colt McCoy can run the ball as well as throw it. Here, he splits the seam between Oklahoma defenders during the 2009 Red River Rivalry game.

Tony Gutierrez, Associated Press

Graceful in defeat, Colt McCoy congratulates Alabama running back Mark Ingram after the University of Alabama won the the BCS Championship Game on January 7, 2010. Ingram's Crimson Tide downed McCoy's Texas Longhorns 37–21, after Colt was injured early in the first quarter.

The Cincinnati Bearcats couldn't stop Tim Tebow in his final collegiate game on January 1, 2010 at the Sugar Bowl in New Orleans. Tim threw for a career-high 482 yards and three touchdowns, and he ran for 51 yards and another score.

Bill Haber, Associated Press

"Three-second evangelism" on Tim Tebow's eye black: Romans 1:16 says, "I am not ashamed of the gospel, because it is the power of God for the salvation of everyone who believes: first for the Jew, then for the Gentile." This verse was his theme for a late-season game in 2009 against Florida International University.
Phil Sandlin, Associated Press

BRONCOS
DENVER

A beaming Tim Tebow meets the Denver media the day after his surprise first-round draft selection by the NFL's Broncos.
Eric Bakke, Associated Press

Invesco

Tim Tebow dives onto a padded cover during a photo shoot for the cover of EA Sports' *NCAA Football 11* video game box.

The Three QBs—Sam Bradford, Colt McCoy, and Tim Tebow (left to right)—huddle up after the 2008 Home Depot/ESPNU College Football Awards ceremony in Lake Buena Vista, Florida.

first saw back on the farm. Tim was heaving the ball 50 yards in the air as a sixth grader, and everyone who saw him throw thought, *Wait until he gets to high school.*

Except Tim was homeschooled. How was he going to play high school football when he wasn't going to *go* to high school?

LEADING A HORSE TO WATER . . .

Boys don't generally love to read, and Tim Tebow was no exception. To fuel his desire to read, Pam had him read biographies of famous athletes and write reports about them. If she could relate a science lesson to sports, she tried that, too.

One time, Tim wrote a report on why athletes' bodies need more protein, which he entered in the local science fair. After winning first place, Tim convinced his mom he needed to drink protein shakes.

"She was a great teacher," Tim said of his mother. "I love listening to her talk, tell stories. She was always a very sweet teacher—it took a lot for her to get frustrated. She's continuing to teach me, even now that I'm in the NFL. She's still teaching me all the time, showing me how to do things, correcting my grammar."

LOOKING UP TO A HERO

One of the things Tim's parents encouraged him to do when he was very young was pick a hero who modeled humility and modesty. They suggested just the person for nine-year-old Tim to emulate: Danny Wuerffel, the University of Florida quarterback who would win the Heisman Trophy in 1996 and lead the Gators to a national championship the same season.

Dad and Mom both graduated from the University of Florida, so the Tebows were Gator fans who occasionally attended some of their football games. Older sister Katie was making plans to enroll there in the fall of 1997. Tim, who slept under a Gator bedspread and had a bathroom that sported a Gator shower curtain, tacked a giant color poster of Danny Wuerffel to his bedroom wall. Before the start of the 1996 season, young Tim enjoyed seeing his hero at Gators Fan Day.

Tim liked how the Florida QB was quick to give God credit and live his life to bring honor to Him. Danny loved quoting Proverbs 3:5–6 to the media: "Trust in the LORD with all your heart and lean not on your own understanding; in all your ways acknowledge him, and he will make your paths straight."

So Tim wanted to be like Danny Wuerffel—and to play quarterback like him. Would he get his chance?

The answer was yes, thanks to a new Florida law that allowed homeschooled children to take part in interscholastic sports. A homeschooling mom named Brenda Dickinson spearheaded a two-year battle in the Florida legislature that ended in 1996 with the passage of a law providing home-educated students with the opportunity to participate on athletic teams at their local schools. In other words, if a child was schooled at home, he or she had to be "accommodated" and couldn't be kept off the interscholastic playing field.

Florida became one of 16 states that allowed home-schooled kids to play varsity sports at a traditional high school. Robby and Peter Tebow took advantage of that opportunity and played high school football at Trinity Christian Academy in Jacksonville, a K–12 school with 450 high school students that was founded in 1967.

When Tim reached ninth grade, he was itching to play at Trinity Christian as well. But Tim didn't start out playing quarterback—at least not at first. The Trinity Christian coach, Verlon Dorminey, looked at Tim's broad-shouldered build and lined him up on the varsity team at tight end on offense and linebacker on defense.

That was okay for his freshman year, but Tim wanted to play quarterback. Quarterbacks were the playmakers, the center of action. If you were going to *beat* the other team, you needed a quarterback who could make plays. Tim wanted to *lead* his team to victory, not depend on someone else making a play.

Coach Dorminey was open to the idea, but he had installed a Wing-T offense that relied heavily on the run. In his system, the quarterback made a lot of handoffs or ran off the option play. Little or no passing. This run-centered offense worked for Dorminey and the team: Trinity Christian won the Florida state championship in its division in 2002.

That's not what Bob Tebow wanted for his son, though. He knew Tim had a special gift for throwing the ball and that he needed to be on a team where he could shine as quarterback. He didn't want his son typecast at tight end or linebacker —grunt positions that take size. Quarterback—the position with the ultimate skill set—was where he needed to be.

If Tim was ever going to play quarterback in high school football, he had to make his move. That's because quarterbacks establish themselves on the varsity team during their sophomore seasons. Maybe they don't get to play that much because a senior or a junior is ahead of them, but they take their place on the depth chart and learn the position on the practice field.

Since Trinity Christian didn't throw the ball—and since Tim didn't go to school there anyway—the Tebows starting shopping around. They found a public high school in nearby St. John's County where the coach, Craig Howard, ran a spread offense and liked to see the ball in the air, not on the ground.

The school was Nease High, and the football team hadn't been winning much. In fact, the Panthers were 2–8 the season before Tim arrived and 1–9 the year before that.

In other words, the perfect situation for Tim Tebow.

"We wanted to give Tim the opportunity to develop his God-given talent and to achieve his lifelong dream of playing quarterback," Bob said. "It wasn't that we were leaving an unsuccessful program to go to a successful one; it was the other way around."

There was just one hitch, though: Tim had to live in the Nease High School district, but the Tebow farm was situated in nearby Duval County.

The Tebows overcame that hurdle by renting an apartment close to Nease High in Ponte Vedra Beach. They put the family farm up for sale and signed up Tim to play football at Nease High. Pam and Tim did Bible studies and worked through his homeschool curriculum in the morning and early afternoon, and then it was off to football practice at Nease High. The family farm never sold, so the Tebows eventually ended up keeping their homestead, but as Bob said, "We were willing to make that sacrifice. We made sacrifices for all our children."

Nease High—named after Allen Duncan Nease, a pioneer of Florida's reforestation and conservation efforts in the mid-twentieth century—was a public high school of about 1,600 students that played in Florida's 4A division.

In Florida—a state that, like Texas and Oklahoma, is a hotbed of high school football talent—schools competed in one of eight classifications, all based on enrollment. The largest classification in the state was 6A, and the smallest was 1B, so there were some schools in Florida classed higher than Nease and many classed lower.

Tim's talent could not be denied nor his work ethic overlooked. Coach Howard certainly noticed. "People can always lead with words but not always with actions," he said. "Timmy was the hardest worker I've ever been around. His work ethic was uncompromising, and all of those around him were affected by it."

Like Sam and Colt, Tim won the starting quarterback role in his sophomore season. Based on their history of losing, though, the Panthers figured to be the patsy on other teams' schedules. "We had six road games my sophomore year, and we were the homecoming game for all six of them," Tim said. "Talk about embarrassing."

But the Panthers, with their sophomore quarterback making throws, bullying his way through the line, and never giving up, acquitted themselves well during Tim's first season there. Nease High finished 5–5 in 2003, a turnaround that portended better things to come.

BREAKOUT TIME

Why do you think Sam, Colt, and Tim had such big junior seasons in high school football? You could say that their maturity and confidence played a big role, but they also needed a strong cast around them to block, catch the ball, and stop the other team from scoring. In that respect, all three were in the right place at the right time as high school juniors.

But think how the situation was different for Tim. He didn't go to school with his teammates. No friendly banter between classes or hanging out in the cafeteria during lunchtime. No horseplay or kidding around while gathering for a school assembly.

Yet Tim won over his teammates with his hard work on the practice field, his unyielding determination to win, and his respectful attitude toward them and the coaches. His teammates saw him as a nice, fun-loving guy—as one of them, even though he didn't go to classes during the school day.

For Tim, all the pieces were in place for a successful 2004 season. He was big and brawny, pushing past 6 feet, 2 inches tall, and weighing in north of 215 pounds. He single-handedly, by force of will and great talent, took a nothing team and turned it into an 11–2 powerhouse that advanced to the third round of the state playoffs.

If Tim wasn't pile-driving his way through the line like a determined fullback, he was hitting receivers between the numbers and lofting bombs into the end zone. Suddenly, rival schools didn't want anything to do with Nease High on homecoming night.

Coach Howard saw that he had a thoroughbred in Tim, and he let him run—and throw and throw and throw. Before the season was over, Tim had set the state record for total yards in a season with 5,576, of which 4,304 yards came from passing (for an average of 331 yards per game). He was also responsible for 70 touchdowns in 13 games—and that's not a typo: he tossed 46 touchdown passes (more than three per game) and ran for 24 more, making himself the ultimate "dual-threat" quarterback. He threw just six interceptions all season.

NO FACE IN THE CROWD

The honors rolled in for Tim Tebow following his junior season: Florida Dairy Farmers Player of the Year, All-State, and a third-place finish in Florida's Mr. Football balloting. He rose up the college recruiting Web sites such as Rivals. com and SuperPrep.com like a hit song on a Top 40 chart. Scout.com even ranked him third nationally among high school quarterback prospects.

Sportswriter John Patton of the *Gainesville Sun* called Tim "the best high school football player I have ever seen"— even though he still had another season of high school ball left. Then, at the end of his junior season, *Sports Illustrated* printed his smiling mug in the magazine's "Faces in the Crowd" section.

The hype machine was pulling out of the driveway.

College coaches descended upon the Tebow family like solicitous salesmen carrying briefcases filled with their wares. Eighty schools offered him scholarships and pleaded with him to come play for State U, but the only ones the Tebows gave active consideration were the University of Miami, the University of Michigan, the University of Southern California, the University of Alabama, and Bob and Pam's alma mater —the University of Florida.

Unlike Sam and Colt, however, the Tebow parents didn't want Tim to make a verbal commitment to any college at the end of his junior year. They weren't ready yet; they wanted to take their time.

As word got around about this Tebow kid in Florida, an ESPN producer smelled a good story and sent a camera crew from Murrah Communications to Nease High during the summer of 2005. Coach Howard gave the film crew full access throughout the 2005 season—training camp, locker room, practice field, and the sidelines during the games. The coach even allowed himself to be miked up.

This would be an ESPN *Faces in Sports* program, and the title of the hour-long documentary was *The Chosen One*. The storyline was Tim's record-setting career at Nease, his senior season, and the team's drive toward a state championship. The program ended with Tim's postseason announcement in December of which school he had chosen to attend.

The Chosen One is still worth watching. (It's readily available in five segments on YouTube.) It's a chance to watch a youthful Tim—wearing a No. 5 jersey—not only develop as a player but also into a young man learning to deal with intense media scrutiny. He handled everything with aplomb. There are many amazing scenes:

- Tim and his dad sitting at the dinner table at their ranch house, sifting through a mound of recruiting letters from the nation's top college football coaches—many handwritten—informing Tim that he'd be a "welcome addition" to their program.
- Pam perched at a small table with Tim in their Ponte Vedra apartment, working through a homeschool lesson together.

- Bob and Pam talking about their years in the Philippines and a clip of Tim preaching before hundreds of Filipino kids when he was only 15 years old.
- Tim in the locker room, firing up his team before a big game like it was the end of the world.
- Tim suffering a broken leg but refusing to be pulled out of the game, and later hobbling 29 yards into the end zone on sheer guts.
- Bob standing in a grassy field, reading Proverbs 22:6 from his Bible ("Train a child in the way he should go . . .").

THE NEXT BIG THING

The cameras were there when Nease High opened the 2005 season with a road game against highly regarded Hoover High in Hoover, Alabama, which aired *nationally* on ESPN. Even though Nease lost 50–29, everyone agreed that Tim put on quite a show.

The national media had now officially anointed Tim as the Next Big Thing. Tim backed that up by putting together another record-breaking season and leading Nease to its first state championship, which the Panthers took home after beating Armwood High 44–37 in the state final. Tim's stats: 237 yards and four touchdowns in the air, 153 yards and two touchdowns on the ground . . . and jokes about selling pop-corn at halftime.

All that was left for Tim to do was to announce which college had won his heart. The family narrowed down the choices to Alabama or Florida, and then Bob and Pam stepped aside. *It's your decision, Son. You're the one who's going to be playing there. You pray about it and let the Lord guide your steps.*

Three days after pocketing the state championship, Tim—dressed in a dark coat, blue shirt, and white tie—took the podium at the Nease High Performing Arts Center. He stood before an auditorium packed with hundreds of screaming teenagers and Gator partisans. ESPN's cameras were there—live.

That morning, Tim and his golden lab, Otis, had gone for a long walk into the pine trees and oaks that outlined their homestead. He sat next to a nearby lake and thought and prayed about what he should do. He and his parents liked both coaches; Urban Meyer at Florida and Mike Shula at Alabama were God-fearing men of strong character. Both schools were capable of winning the national title. This was one of those win-win decisions.

In the end, the edge went to Florida. Coach Meyer ran a spread offense, just like Coach Howard did at Nease, and the family's deep roots at the University of Florida couldn't be glossed over. Mom and Dad went there, and Pam's father had played basketball there. Tim had grown up in Gator Nation. The school was close to home, which meant his parents and siblings—Team Tebow—could watch him play at Ben Hill Griffin Stadium, a.k.a. "The Swamp."

Bob and Pam held their breath as Tim straddled the podium, looked straight into the camera, and said, "I will be playing college football next year at the University of Florida."

THE GREEN SHIRT AT GATOR NATION
How do you describe the four-year college career that

launched Tebowmania and lifted Tim into the living rooms of millions of Americans?

Do you start with Tim's freshman year and his double-pump "jump pass" for a one-yard touchdown against LSU that had announcers raving about his originality? Or was it the *Braveheart* scene at Florida State—when Tim's face and white jersey were smeared in the "war paint" from the end zone? Or how about the controversy when he started inscribing Bible verses on his eye black?

When Tim announced, "I will be playing college football next year at the University of Florida," he was talking about playing the very *next* season, not kicking back and enjoy a low-stress redshirt year. In January 2006, within a few weeks of his announcement, Tim enrolled at Florida. He didn't have to wait to graduate with his high school class—he *was* the class.

Tim was eligible to enroll in college because he had completed his studies and had taken an SAT test in ninth grade. By becoming a University of Florida student, Tim made himself eligible to participate in spring football practice—the rehearsal time for the fall season.

In the college football lexicon, he was not a red shirt but a "green shirt"—green as in "go early." A green-shirt athlete is someone who graduates from high school in December of his senior year and immediate enrolls in college so he can participate in spring practice—and get a head start on learning the system and moving up the depth chart.

Chris Leak was a senior and a three-year starter for the Gators, so he was the No. 1 quarterback. But Tim wasn't willing to rock on his cleats on the Florida sidelines, helmet in hand, waiting for his chance to play. He was going to *compete* for the job, even as a true freshman.

At the annual Orange and Blue scrimmage game, which ended three weeks of spring practice, Tim looked sharp in leading his Orange team to a 24–6 victory. "Chris Leak is our quarterback, and Tim Tebow is a guy who is going to play," Coach Meyer said afterward. "There is no quarterback controversy. There are two great young men who we are going to build an offense around to be successful."

Translation: *We're going to start Chris Leak so our freshman quarterback doesn't have the pressure of being the starter, but he's going to be playing a lot.*

Tim did play a lot as a true freshman in 2006, even though Florida had arguably the toughest schedule in the nation. He scored the first time he touched the ball in a Florida uniform—on a goal-line keeper against Southern Mississippi. Coach Meyer continued to play Tim in spot situations, bringing him along slowly. But in the third game of the season, against Tennessee—in Knoxville, before 106,818 rabid Volunteer fans—Meyer threw Tim into the fire. In the fourth quarter, with the Gators trailing by six points, Florida faced a fourth-and-one inside Tennessee territory. Meyer flung Tim into the game, Tim punched out two yards to keep the drive alive, and Chris Leak took his place and led the Gators to the winning score.

Against Southeastern Conference opponents, Florida fell into a familiar pattern throughout the season—fall behind early, then claw its way back. Against LSU, Tim unveiled his first "jump pass." With Florida knocking on the door at the one yard line, Tim took the snap five yards behind center, ran toward the pile, then suddenly leaped and lobbed a rainbow pass to his tight end, Tate Casey. Touchdown!

It was a clever play—known in the Florida playbook as Trey Left, 341 Stop Bend X Fake—that hadn't been seen since the days of Bronko Nagurski and leather helmets. With retro panache, Tim would make two more jump passes in his career at Florida. (Heads up, NFL defenses.)

After defeating LSU, Florida—now ranked No. 2 in the country—suffered its first hiccup of the season—against Auburn in a 27–17 road loss in an ESPN *GameDay* match-up. A controversial fourth-quarter fumble by Chris Leak, with Florida trailing 21–17 but driving for the potential win, sealed the Gators' fate.

That was the only smudge on an otherwise golden 2006 Florida football season. The Gators ran the table the rest of the way, beating Georgia, Florida State, and Arkansas (in the SEC Championship Game) to climb back to No. 2 in the polls and into the BCS National Championship Game—played at the new University of Phoenix Stadium in Glendale, Arizona—against top-ranked Ohio State.

Florida thrashed the Buckeyes 41–14 to win its second national football championship in school history—the other one happening in 1996 when Danny Wuerffel was the Gator quarterback. The victory also helped mark the first time in college sports history that the NCAA college basketball and football titles rested in the same trophy case—the Gator men's basketball team having won the national championship in the spring of 2006. Chris Leak played clutch football, and when Tim spelled him, he found the soft spots in the Ohio State defense with his power running, scoring one touchdown and throwing for another on college football's biggest night.

At a well-attended victory celebration at Ben Hill Griffin Stadium a few days later, a special guest was invited onstage to hand Chris Leak the Most Valuable Player trophy. Who was the surprise invitee?

Danny Wuerffel, Tim's boyhood hero.

After telling Chris they were now the only starting Gator quarterbacks in Florida football history to bear national championship rings, Danny paused for a moment and turned to the freshman quarterback standing nearby. Everyone wondered what Danny Wonderful would say.

"There's room for another one next year, Timmy Tebow," he said.

The baton had been officially passed.

IT'S TIM'S TEAM NOW

With Chris Leak graduated, the Florida Gators were now Tim Tebow's team. Everyone knew it. A FLORIDA FOLK HERO PREPARES TO FACE REALITY read a preseason headline in the *New York Times,* which knew an important story when it saw one.

The story noted that during the offseason, Tim had sung "She Thinks My Tractor's Sexy" on stage with country singer Kenny Chesney, preached in two prisons "so convincingly" that 200 hardened criminals began weeping and became Christians, and dealt with coeds camping outside his apartment—some who asked him to autograph their underwear.

Saying that Tim had a big year in 2007, after having just turned 19 years of age, would be like saying the New York Yankees and Murderer's Row had a big year in 1927. The way

Tim performed in 2007 was remarkable, considering these developments:

- He played much of the season with a severely bruised shoulder.
- Some of his teammates weren't as committed, didn't play as well as the graduated seniors from the 2006 team, or got themselves into trouble off the field or in the classroom.
- Tim's roommate, Tony Joiner, was arrested for breaking into a Gainesville tow lot and attempting to retrieve his girlfriend's impounded car. Though it was a misunderstanding and the charges were later dropped, Coach Meyer stripped Joiner of his role as team captain.
- Tim's offensive coordinator, Dan Mullen, underwent an emergency appendectomy less than 24 hours before he called Florida's offensive plays in the Gators' 20–17 loss to Auburn. (Tim called his coach a "warrior" for being at the game right after the procedure.)
- Tim fractured his right hand in a late-season game against Florida State but continued playing anyway (remember, he throws left-handed). He would wear a cast for the next three weeks.

Tim hurdled those bumps in the road like he ran over defenses—like they were just little nuisances. And the numbers he put up!

In the season opener against Western Kentucky, Tim led the Gators to touchdowns on their first four possessions. He finished his first career start by going 13-for-17 for 300 yards with three touchdown passes and one rushing touchdown in a 49–3 wipeout. Another warm-up game against Troy was also a Tebow gem.

Tim's first big test as a starter was the 2007 SEC opener against Tennessee, which was played before 90,707 hot and sticky fans at The Swamp. Tim was unstoppable, running and throwing the ball up and down the field almost at will. When he scored on a seven-yard touchdown run in the second quarter, CBS cameras caught safety and roommate Tony Joiner planting a kiss on Tim's left cheek as a reward.

The lovefest continued until Tim's first interception of the season, which resulted in a 93-yard Volunteer touchdown to pull Tennessee to within 28–20 in the third quarter. After that, though, the rout was on—31 unanswered Florida points as Tim racked up 61 yards on the ground and 299 yards through the air.

A nice Big Orange smoothie.

After the Tennessee game, the *Gainesville Sun* collected the best quotes from others about Tim Tebow:

Lou Holtz, ESPN analyst: "Florida just has so many playmakers, including that Superman who plays quarterback."

Gary Parrish, CBSSports.com: "And so his first league start was laced with such curiosity, and a national television audience turned to CBS to see what exactly this poster boy of a signal caller could do against Tennessee. Now, everybody is just wondering what he can't do. Against Tennessee or anybody else."

Stewart Mandel, SI.com: "QB Tim Tebow exceeded even the most delusional expectations in his first SEC start."

Dave Hyde, South Florida *Sun-Sentinel*: "Of all things

good and great you could say about Tebow, the best is this: he is living up to the hype, the hoopla, the borderline non-sense as represented by the 'Tebow is God' and 'Tebow for President' signs hanging Saturday from student houses by the stadium."

HE15MAN TIME

This amalgamation of Joe Montana and Jim Brown added up to two words: *Tebow hysteria*. Some zealous Florida fans created TimTebowFacts.com, where fans could contribute a list of Tim's most legendary, Paul Bunyanesque accomplishments. T-shirt makers started silkscreening "He15man" on Gator blue shirts, and the ESPN and CBS football pundits declared that Tim was the early-season favorite for the Heisman Trophy, even though they were careful to insert a "but"—*but a sophomore has never won the Heisman, Lou*. They pointed out that ex-Gator quarterback Rex Grossman didn't win one in 2001 and running back Darren McFadden of Arkansas didn't pick up the Heisman in 2006, even though both players had superb seasons, so it was likely never to happen.

Tim's legend expanded the following week against Ole Miss when he took over a road game in Oxford, Mississippi, that Florida looked destined to lose. The Gators struggled most of the game until five consecutive Tebow runs set up a short field goal that gave the Gators a 30–24 lead with less than five minutes to play. After a stop, when Florida needed to run time off the clock, Tim carried the ball six consecutive times to secure a victory and keep the No. 3 Gators undefeated for the season. In all, Tim accounted for all four Gator touchdowns and 427 of his team's 507 total yards.

But the Gators lost three of their next four games, falling to Auburn at home, LSU in Baton Rouge, and Georgia at the neutral Jacksonville site. Tim didn't do much against Georgia because of a right shoulder contusion he suffered the previous week against Kentucky. When he was in the game, the Georgia rush menaced him the entire afternoon, sacking him six times. It seemed like he was running for his life the entire game.

Tim, who had wiped tears from his face after walking off the field at LSU, had to fight back moisture in his eyes at the postgame podium as he faced the media following the tough loss to interstate rival Georgia. "I do take them [the losses] hard," he said, "but that's because I am so passionate."

Listening to the Georgia game on her computer, via the Internet, was his sister Christy. It was the middle of the night in Bangladesh, where she had recently moved with her husband, Joey, and their one-year-old daughter, Claire, to do missionary work.

After the game, Tim spoke by phone with Christy, who told him how she and her family were adjusting to life in one of the poorest countries of the world. He felt chastened. "It makes you realize that everything that happens in this game doesn't really mean that much in the grand scheme of things," Tim said. "Losing to Georgia is not the biggest thing in the world."

The Gators—and Tim—bounced back and played a perfect November, even though his shoulder bruise still bothered him. He shook off the pain and ran for five touchdowns against South Carolina, set a career-best in passing yards with 338 against Florida Atlantic, and dominated intrastate

rival Florida State at The Swamp, despite suffering a dis-
placed fracture on his non-throwing right hand. He played
30 downs with the busted hand and laid out his final argu-
ment to win the Heisman Trophy. In the closing moments
of a one-sided 45–12 victory against the Seminoles, Gator
cheerleaders struck Heisman poses—carriage slightly bent,
leg up, right arms thrust out to stiff-arm a tackler—on the
sidelines.

Florida finished the season a respectable 9–3 and earned
a January 1, 2008, date with Michigan at the Citrus Bowl. But
the big story in Gator Nation was whether Tim would capture the Heisman Trophy.

In the 72-year history of the award, Heisman voters—
sportswriters and past winners—had never handed the award
to a sophomore, reserving the honor for upperclassmen. It
seemed to be one of those unwritten rules.

Wait your turn, son.

But who had played better than Tim Tebow in 2007? Some
said Arkansas running back Darren McFadden deserved it
after failing to strike the pose in 2006, or that University of
Hawaii senior quarterback Colt Brennan should win because
of his outlandish passing stats, but no one played better than
Tim in 2007.

In early December, Tim and his family flew to New York
City for the Heisman Trophy ceremony at the Nokia Theatre
in Times Square. It turned out to be a family reunion when
Christy and her family flew to New York from Bangladesh—
the first time Team Tebow had been all together since the
previous Christmas. The family was overjoyed.

When he heard his name announced as the winner, a

beaming Tim bound up out of his chair and hugged his parents, then Gator coach Urban Meyer. Standing on the stage with all the surviving Heisman winners since 1935 was his boyhood idol, Danny Wuerffel, who greeted him with another hug.

After first thanking God for the ability to play football, Tim thanked his teammates back home, his coaches, and especially his parents: "I want to thank my dad, who taught me a work ethic every day growing up, and my mom, who instilled in me so many great characters."

It's okay, Tim. This was live TV before millions of viewers. We know what you meant: Mom instilled in you so many great characteristics.

Afterward, he told interviewers, "I think it's amazing that you're known forever as a Heisman Trophy winner. That's very special. It's overwhelming. I'm kind of at a loss for words." Football commentators agreed that being the first NCAA Division 1 quarterback ever to have a "20/20" season—22 rushing touchdowns and 29 touchdown passes—sealed the deal with Heisman voters.

Tim, the youngest Heisman winner ever at 20 years of age, accepted the trophy with a blue cast on his right hand, one year before another sophomore, Sam Bradford, would hold the same trophy with a red cast protecting his surgically repaired left thumb.

The 2007 season ended with a 41–35 loss to Michigan on New Year's Day. Tim played with a soft cast to protect his mending right hand. Although the defeat was disappointing to the Gators and their fans, they knew Tim would be returning the following season—all healed up and with a talented, more experienced team surrounding him.

Deep within, a passion burned within Tim for a national championship ring—the one Danny Wuerffel said there was room for.

PROMISE MADE, PROMISE KEPT

In Gator lore, it's called "The Promise."

Here's the situation. Through the first three games of the 2008 season, Florida was pancaking opponents. Victories over Hawaii, Miami, and Tennessee were as lopsided as some girls' basketball games. The talk in Gator Nation was that this team could go undefeated—something never done in the history of Florida football.

Ole Miss was coming into Gainesville a decided underdog—22 points according to the odds makers. Quarterbacking the Rebels was Jevan Snead, who (1) "decommitted" to Florida after Tim announced he would become a Gator and (2) enrolled at Texas but transferred to Ole Miss after getting beat out by Colt McCoy. So you could excuse Snead if he had a bit of an inferiority complex playing in Tim Tebow's house.

But Snead was a gamer, as was the entire Rebel team. They made plays, recovered fumbles from Tim and star running back Percy Harvin, and "hung around"—football-speak for a team that should have been put away after falling behind 17–7.

The game was tied 24–24 midway through the fourth quarter when the Rebels—playing with house money since they were still in the game—got lucky (if you're a Gator fan) or made a great effort (if you're an Ole Miss fan). Snead found

Shay Hodge all alone on the sideline for an 86-yard scoring play to give Ole Miss a 31–24 lead with 5:26 to play.

Tim and the Gators hitched up their pants and scored quickly when Percy Harvin scooted 15 yards for a touchdown. The extra point attempt, however, was blocked when an Ole Miss player hurdled a blocker to tip the kick—an illegal tactic in organized football. Coach Meyer argued his case but to no avail.

Disaster! Instead of being tied, Florida was down 31–30. With 3:28 left, the Florida defense needed a quick stop, which it got. Tim had the offense driving, but the Gators faced a fourth-and-one on the Ole Miss 32-yard line. Do you go for a 49-yard field goal to win the game or get the first down and try to get closer?

The Gators were going for it—but the Rebel defense stuffed Tim at the line of scrimmage.

Game over.

When Tim faced the media afterward, he was asked if he wanted to forget the loss. "I don't want to," an emotional Tim replied. "I want it to stay in our hearts and keep hurting so that we'll never let this happen again."

Then he paused and gathered his thoughts. What spilled forth was what came to be known as "The Promise":

> "I just want to say one thing" . . . *deep breath* . . . "to the fans and everybody in Gator Nation" . . . *pause, sniffle* . . . "I'm sorry. I'm extremely sorry. We were hoping for an undefeated season. That was my goal, something Florida's never done here.
>
> "I promise you one thing: a lot of good will come

out of this. You will never see any player in the entire country who will play as hard as I will play the rest of the season. You will never see someone push the rest of the team as hard as I will push everybody the rest of the season.

"You will never see a team play harder than we will the rest of the season. God bless."

With that, Tim exited the postgame podium—and Florida didn't lose another game the rest of the 2008 season.

THREE-SECOND EVANGELISM

Two weeks after the Ole Miss debacle, Tim took the field against LSU suited up like he always was for a home game: blue-jersey-and-white-pants Gator uniform, football pads, cleats, and a helmet. Underneath his eyes, on his upper cheeks, were two black rectangular patches.

Called "eye black," this dark mixture of beeswax, paraffin, and carbon is applied under the eyes to reduce glare. Sunlight or stadium lights can impair the view of an airborne ball.

Tim began wearing smudges of eye black during Florida day games, but before this important test against the defending national champion LSU Tigers, he had someone in the locker room use a white grease pencil to print **PHL** on top of the black strip underneath his right eye and **4:13** under the left eye. The idea was an out-of-the-box, genuine, and clever way to share the biblical message of Philippians 4:13—"I can do all things through Christ who strengthens me"—with millions of football viewers.

Remember, the camera loved Tim Tebow. Throughout the

game, TV producers in the truck inserted as many close-up "cutaways" of Tim as they could—like when he was barking out signals in the shotgun or swallowing a spritz of Gatorade on the Florida sideline with his helmet off.

Tim wasn't the first player to write a message on his eye black. A few years earlier, USC running back Reggie Bush printed "619" on both rectangular swatches—the area code of his hometown of San Diego.

The eye-black-with-a-Bible-verse-story took on a life of its own after the LSU victory, and for every game during the rest of his college career, Tim "shared" a Bible verse with his football-watching audience.

Talk about three-second evangelism. These spiritual billboards sent millions to their Bibles or to their computers to find out what the Bible verse of the week said. What Tim did with his eye black messages was share his Christian faith, jumpstart a national conversation—and add to his legend.

Tim took some hits from the media, though. "There's something strange about the alliance of modern sports and religion," a columnist with *The Tennessean* opined. Others felt religion and sports should not mix. "Why must he rub it in my face?" was the sentiment of *Orlando Sentinel*'s David Whitley.

None of the potshots fazed Tim or changed the way he played throughout the rest of the 2008 season. After "The Promise," he actually accomplished what he pledged to do: grab his team by the scruff of the neck and yank them over the national championship goal line.

Look how lopsided these victories were following the Ole Miss loss:

- Arkansas, 38–7
- LSU, 51–21
- Kentucky, 63–5
- Georgia, 49–10
- Vanderbilt, 42–14
- South Carolina, 56–6
- The Citadel, 70–19
- Florida State, 45–15

The eight-game winning streak earned fourth-ranked Florida a date with No. 1-ranked Alabama for the SEC Championship. Alabama was a solid 10-point favorite for this monster match-up in Atlanta.

With star running back Percy Harvin out of the game, an even heavier offensive load fell on Tim's shoulders. The way he took over in the fourth quarter with his team down 20–17, engineering two touchdown drives, ranked right up at the top of the Tebow highlight reel. He kept the chains moving by throwing into tight spots and battering the 'Bama defense with muscular runs.

"You knew he was going to lead us to victory," said receiver Carl Moore following a 31–20 triumph that catapulted the Gators into the BCS National Championship Game against top-ranked Oklahoma. "You looked into his eyes, and you could see he was intense. We were all intense."

A HEISMAN REPEAT?

After the Alabama conquest, Tim learned he was again a finalist for the Heisman Trophy, so he and his family repeated the trip to Manhattan. This time around at the Nokia Theatre, he was the first to hug Sam Bradford after the Sooner quarterback's name was announced as college football's most outstanding player.

Tim did receive plenty of recognition for his stellar 2008 season—like the Maxwell Award and the Manning Award—but none meant more to him than taking a phone call from Danny Wuerffel, who informed Tim that he'd won the 2008 Wuerffel Trophy, presented annually to the college football player who combines exemplary community service with athletic and academic achievement.

After retiring from professional football in 2004, Danny and his family joined Desire Street Ministries in one of New Orleans' toughest and poorest neighborhoods.

"He's just an amazing young man, an amazing football player," Danny said. "It's funny how things go back and forth. Maybe one day my son will win the Tebow Trophy."

CHAMPIONSHIP GAME MOTIVATION

Florida had one month to prepare for the national championship game, which felt very much like a home game to the Gators since they would be playing the Sam Bradford-led Oklahoma Sooners at Dolphins Stadium in Miami. What made the matchup even more intriguing was that Florida and Oklahoma had *never* played each other before.

Tim didn't have to reach too deep to summon pregame motivation. The acrid smell of the September defeat to Ole Miss still singed his nostrils, and losing the Heisman Trophy vote, despite winning more first-place votes (309 to 300) than Sam Bradford, certainly smarted. And when Sooners cornerback Dominique Franks popped off that Tim would probably be the fourth-best quarterback in the Big 12 Conference—

well, that's all the incentive Tim needed in his wheelhouse.

Thus, properly inspired, Tim decided to forgo **EPH 4:31** and inscribe his eye black with the most widely quoted Bible verse—and one considered the summary of the most central doctrine in Christianity—**John 3:16**:

> "For God so loved the world that he gave his one and only Son, that whoever believes in him shall not perish but have eternal life."

Once the BCS championship game started, though, Tim was out of sync—like Superman without his cape. Two interceptions came on balls he shouldn't have thrown. The Oklahoma defense swarmed the line of scrimmage and shut down Tim as well as the Gator ground game. Florida scored only one touchdown in the first half, which would normally put a team in a big hole against a team like Oklahoma, a juggernaut that averaged 50 points a game and rarely had to send their punt team onto the field. But the Gator defense was up to the challenge, and the score was tied 7–7 at halftime.

The Florida defense continued making big stops after intermission, and then Tim got into the flow, converting several big third downs by running and throwing to stake Florida to a small lead. Tim then put a cherry atop the BCS championship sundae when he lobbed a four-yard jump pass to David Nelson with 3:07 left in the game, giving Florida a commanding 24–14 lead.

After a four-down stop, all the Florida offense had to do was run out the clock. An exuberant Tim got a bit over-the-top when he celebrated a big 13-yard rush by aiming a "Gator

Chomp" at Oklahoma's Nic Harris. Tim fully extended his arms, one above the other, and then moved them together and apart to symbolize the opening and closing of an alligator's mouth. An official threw a yellow flag in the air for taunting, and Florida was penalized 15 yards.

"I was pretty excited," Tim said after the game. "Just gave it a little Gator Chomp, and it was also for the fans. I think they kind of enjoyed it." Gator fans also enjoyed how Tim made "The Promise" come true. Everyone on the Florida team believed the Ole Miss loss turned around the season.

Funny how a loss can turn out to be a blessing in more ways than one.

And on a side note, Google reported that searches for "John 3:16" totaled 93 million during and immediately after the BCS victory by Florida.

"I'M COMING BACK"

After the national championship-clinching win over Oklahoma, a plaque was affixed to the James W. "Bill" Heavener Football Complex outside The Swamp. Entitled "The Promise," the silver tablet immortalized Tim's emotional postgame speech following the Ole Miss loss.

The idea to mount Tim's heartfelt declaration came from Coach Meyer, who thought Tim's words would inspire future generations of Gators, much the same way Knute Rockne's "Win one for the Gipper" speech back in 1928 had ignited Notre Dame teams over the decades.

Quite an honor—especially for a college football player with one season left to play. Or was Tim bolting to the NFL? He was eligible to turn pro.

"Let's do it again!" he shouted to an estimated 42,000 Gator fans celebrating the team's national championship at The Swamp three days after the victory in Miami. "I'm coming back!"

A few days later, *Sports Illustrated*'s cover showed Tim about to slap his palms in that infamous Gator Chomp against Oklahoma. The headline: Not Done Yet: Two Titles in Three Years, and Tim Tebow Is Coming Back for More.

Tim never thought seriously about passing up his senior year to go play in the NFL, but he *did* start giving a great deal of thought to what Bible verses he would inscribe on his eye black during his final season of college football. Before each game in 2009, Tim lettered a new Bible verse on his eye black, sending millions of fans to their computers to do a Google search.

Here's a list of the opponents and the verses Tim wore on his eye black:

Charleston Southern: Proverbs 3:5–6
Trust in the Lord with all your heart and lean not on your own understanding; in all your ways acknowledge him, and he will make your paths straight.

Troy: Mark 8:36
"What good is it for a man to gain the whole world, yet forfeit his soul?"

Tennessee: Romans 8:28
And we know that in all things God works for the good of those who love him, who have been called according to his purpose.

Kentucky: Isaiah 40:31

But those who hope in the LΟRD *will renew their strength. They will soar on wings like eagles; they will run and not grow weary, they will walk and not be faint.*

LSU: 1 Thessalonians 5:18

Give thanks in all circumstances, for this is God's will for you in Christ Jesus.

Arkansas: Psalm 23:1

The LΟRD *is my shepherd, I shall not be in want.*

Mississippi State: Ephesians 4:32

Be kind and compassionate to one another, forgiving each other, just as in Christ God forgave you.

Georgia: Philippians 4:6–7

Do not be anxious about anything, but in everything, by prayer and petition, with thanksgiving, present your requests to God. And the peace of God, which transcends all understanding, will guard your hearts and your minds in Christ Jesus.

Vanderbilt: Colossians 3:23

Whatever you do, work at it with all your heart, as working for the Lord, not for men.

South Carolina: Joshua 1:8–9

"Do not let this Book of the Law depart from your mouth; meditate on it day and night, so that you may

be careful to do everything written in it. Then you will be prosperous and successful. Have I not commanded you? Be strong and courageous. Do not be terrified; do not be discouraged, for the LORD your God will be with you wherever you go."

Florida International: Romans 1:16
I am not ashamed of the gospel, because it is the power of God for the salvation of everyone who believes: first for the Jew, then for the Gentile.

Florida State: Hebrews 12:1–2
Therefore, since we are surrounded by such a great cloud of witnesses, let us throw off everything that hinders and the sin that so easily entangles, and let us run with perseverance the race marked out for us. Let us fix our eyes on Jesus, the author and perfecter of our faith, who for the joy set before him endured the cross, scorning its shame, and sat down at the right hand of the throne of God.

It turned out Bob Tebow got a preacher after all.

A FAREWELL AT THE SWAMP

For Tim's final home game, against Florida State—Senior Day—Gator fans were urged to wear eye black, with or without an inscribed Bible verse. After Florida whipped its intrastate rival, the Gators had a sparkling 12–0 regular season record, had been ranked No.1 all season, and were two games away from completing the program's first-ever perfect season.

The stage was set for back-to-back national champion-ships, but first there was some business to conduct against Alabama in the SEC Championship Game, a rematch from the year before held in Atlanta's Georgia Dome.

This time, it was all Crimson Tide. The Florida defense allowed Alabama to convert on 11 of 15 third-down oppor-tunities, which kept the Tide rolling down the field and chew-ing up the game possession clock. Alabama's offense was on the field for 39 minutes, 27 seconds, nearly 20 minutes longer than Florida.

Instead of giving the Tide a hard-fought game early on, the Gators went meekly into the night, losing 32–13. Their 22-game win streak was toast, and the dream of a perfect sea-son was rudely ended.

The enduring image from that game is Tim bent down on one knee with his team hopelessly behind by three touch-downs as the clock ticks away, the tears streaming through his eye black and down his face. He barely held it together during a postgame interview with CBS' sideline reporter, Tracy Wolfson.

"Tim Tearbow" is how some bloggers lit him up, but Tim had one game left in his college career—a January 1 date with No. 5 Cincinnati in the Sugar Bowl.

LOW THROW

If you look at Tim's performance at the 2010 Sugar Bowl, you would think he single-handedly destroyed the Bearcats. He put on a passing exhibition, completing his first 12 passes and going 20-for-23 in the first half for 320 yards and three touchdowns. When it was all over, he had torched Cincinnati for 482 passing yards and supplied the perfect ending to a storied four-year career. The 51–24 annihilation of the previously unbeaten Bearcats left Florida as the only BCS team ever to win at least 13 games in back-to-back seasons.

You'd think that Tim would be carried off the field and hailed by the media as one of the greatest college quarterbacks ever. Team Tebow, however, woke up the next day to a media drumbeat that started as a whisper but gained concussive force almost overnight: *Tim Tebow is not first-round draft material for the National Football League. In fact, he should consider a position change to tight end.*

In other words, back to the future.

Here's what happened:

With the Sugar Bowl game out of hand, the Fox commentators in the booth, Thom Brennaman and former Baltimore Ravens coach Brian Billick, tossed the topic of Tim's future into the air and batted it around between beer commercials—oops, during lulls in the action.

Does Tim have what it takes to "play at the next level" and become an NFL quarterback?

Cue up the slo-mo of Tim dropping back to pass.

Using a telestrator, Billick dissected Tim's passing motion like a high school biology teacher peeling back the innards of a frog. "You're going to have to change everything he does," the former Ravens coach declared. "He has a windup delivery. He carries the ball too low. And he needs to read his progressions. He's a helluva player, but how do you make him a first-round pick when you have to change so much?"

Billick's critique certainly made for interesting TV: a former NFL coach slicing up a legendary college player in the midst of the most dominating performance of his career. But what Billick did was bring to light the whispering campaign among NFL general managers and their coaching staffs about Tim's throwing motion—the elongated swoop of his left arm prior to releasing the ball.

The conventional wisdom among NFL cognoscenti was hardening like spackle compound. If Tim wasn't worth a first-round pick in the 2010 NFL draft, was he capable of even playing quarterback at the professional level?

4

PLENTY OF PREDRAFT DRAMA

The instant the 2010 Sugar Bowl game clock struck 00:00, Chase Heavener, who was standing on the floor of the New Orleans Superdome, turned on his Canon 5D Mark II camera—capable of shooting high-quality digital video.

Chase, the son of Bill Heavener (whom the Heavener Football Complex next to The Swamp is named after), was initializing work on a documentary about Tim's road to the NFL. Filming couldn't start until Tim's college career was officially over—to preserve his amateur status—so Chase and his small film crew patiently waited for the final seconds to tick off the Superdome scoreboard. The young filmmaker planned to produce a film about Tim's life from the end of the Sugar Bowl through his first game in the NFL.

It looked like there would be enough drama between the Sugar Bowl and the 2010 NFL draft to fill a miniseries. Tim's opening episode began with the Senior Bowl—a postseason college football exhibition game for graduating seniors played in Mobile, Alabama, in late January. With National Football League coaches and personnel monitoring a week of practices as well as the game, the Senior Bowl would be a showcase for the best prospects in the upcoming NFL draft.

Tim opted to play in the Senior Bowl because he wanted to improve his deteriorating draft standing. Following the Sugar Bowl, NFL scouts were telling reporters—anonymously —that Tim figured to go in the third round and might have to think about playing tight end or H-back, a combination tight end/fullback position. Since Tim wasn't ready to abandon his dream of playing quarterback in the NFL—a yearning of his since he was six years old—he didn't shy away from a week of Senior Bowl practices . . . or from working on his ball placement, footwork, and release.

Team Tebow was aware of the NFL's reservations about his mechanics and loopy throwing motion. In fact, he made the decision to reinvent himself *before* the Senior Bowl by attending the D1 Sports Training facility in Cool Springs, Tennessee, outside Nashville. Tim was one of 18 former college players working out with D1's coaches and trainers. Another one of those former college players was Jordan Shipley, Colt McCoy's best friend and favorite receiver at Texas.

Tim had visited several other training facilities before deciding on D1, which was co-owned by Indianapolis Colts quarterback Peyton Manning. Waiting for him were several experienced coaches: Marc Trestman, a former quarterbacks coach with Tampa Bay, Cleveland, and Minnesota; Zeke Bratkowski, a longtime NFL coach; former NFL head coach Sam Wyche; and current Arizona State University offensive coordinator Noel Mazzone.

THE ROAD TO A REALLY SUPER SUNDAY

As Chase Heavener and his small film crew patiently waited for the final seconds to tick off the Superdome scoreboard at the 2010 Sugar Bowl, there was another group of film people loitering in New Orleans that night—this one from Focus on the Family. They were in the Big Easy to discuss the latest developments regarding a 30-second commercial featuring Tim and his mother that would air during the Super Bowl.

Perhaps you heard about it.

In early 2009, Mark Waters, the head of film production at Focus on the Family—a nonprofit Christian organization that offers practical biblical advice on marriage, parenting, and life challenges—had a brainstorm. He envisioned Pam Tebow sharing the story about her son's miraculous birth in an engaging, upbeat way that would be posted as a video on the ministry's Web site.

Waters pitched the idea to Focus on the Family president Jim Daly, who loved what he heard. *But what about taking the concept a step further? What about involving Tim in the story and turning this into a 30-second commercial? Better yet, a commercial that would run during the Super Bowl. Not only would we generate a buzz, but we could impact the culture with a pro-life message rarely heard in the mainstream media.*

Running a commercial during the Super Bowl is the costliest "ad buy" of the year, running upwards of $3 million for 30 measly seconds—but there are 100 million sets of eyeballs looking in. The Super Bowl is probably the only televised show where viewers *don't* switch the channel during a "commercial time-out" because they know advertisers unveil their cleverest and newest advertisements during breaks in football's biggest game of the year.

Phone calls were made, and a dozen supporters of the

Focus on the Family ministry said they would step up and pay the $2.5 million price tag to air a 30-second ad. The next step was to see if the Tebows were on board.

Jim Daly and Ken Windebank, Focus' senior vice president of public affairs, flew to Jacksonville in the fall to float the idea past Bob and Pam. The Tebows signaled their interest and said they were open to the concept.

Back in Colorado, Mark Waters created two different mock-ups of the commercial and hired actors to play the roles of Pam and Tim Tebow. Then he, Jim Daly, and Ken Windebank traveled to New Orleans to show the Tebow family the run-throughs the day after the Sugar Bowl.

The entire Tebow family, including Tim, watched both mock-ups, transfixed by what they saw. They were emotionally moved and said they were extremely grateful that Pam's story of how she chose life for Tim could be shared in a mighty way. They were grateful to the Lord that this 30-second film would be viewed by millions watching the Super Bowl.

On Tuesday, January 12, everyone met at a soundstage at Full Sail Studios in Winter Park, Florida, just outside Orlando. Pam and Tim looked natural as they spoke their lines in front of a white seamless background. Then Bob and Pam sat in director's chairs opposite Jim Daly for a friendly chat while the video cameras whirred. They shared how they prayed for "Timmy" by name before he was conceived, what it was like to deal with a crisis pregnancy in the Philippines, and why they decided to go forward with the pregnancy—even though Pam's life was in danger and she was urged to have an abortion.

Bob passionately described his vow to God that he would raise Timmy to be a preacher if he survived this "miracle birth." He closed with an emotional plea to women contemplating an abortion: "God loves you and your baby. There are lots of people that will help you. Don't kill your baby."

The plan was to make the Tebows' long-form interview available on the Focus on the Family Web site after the Super Bowl spot aired. The Web address would be displayed at the end of the ad along with the tagline "Celebrate family. Celebrate life."

When the filming was completed, Focus on the Family announced in a January 15 press release that the Tebows had decided to participate in a Super Bowl ad "because the issue of life is one they feel strongly about." CBS—the broadcasting network for the upcoming February 7 Super Bowl—had approved the advertisement based on the test commercial.

With that benign statement, the Tebows tipped over a hornet's nest. Hearing the howls of protest by women's groups in favor of "choice" and "reproductive freedom," you would have thought the end of Western civilization was imminent. The National Organization of Women (NOW), the Feminist Majority, and Women's Media Center called on CBS to scrap the Tebow Super Bowl ad because it was likely to convey an anti-abortion message. NOW labeled the ad "extraordinarily offensive and demeaning." GLAAD, a gay advocacy group, accused CBS of a double standard for rejecting a gay dating site ad and accepting the Focus spot.

No one, of course, had viewed the ad, which wouldn't be shown until Super Sunday.

With the benefit of hindsight, which is always 20/20, the outrage over the Tebows' Super Bowl ad seems rather silly at this point.

In the weeks leading up to the Super Bowl, however, more than 30 women's advocacy groups pressured CBS to drop the ad—*even though none had seen the 30-second spot.* Those who *had* viewed the ad prior to Super Sunday tried to tell anyone who would listen that there was nothing political or controversial about it. "When the day arrives," said Focus on the Family spokesman Gary Schneeberger, "and you sit down and watch the game on TV, those who oppose it will be quite surprised at what the ad is all about."

Focus president Jim Daly tried to say the same thing when he appeared on the *Larry King Live* show six days before the Super Bowl. In a panel discussion, he made an offer to Terry O'Neill, president of NOW: "When you see the ad in the Super Bowl, if you don't like it, I'll buy you lunch."

It's likely that Jim Daly never heard from Terry O'Neill after the Super Bowl.

Like a brilliant fake in the open field, the Tebow ad left detractors flummoxed, flat-footed, and gasping for air. The national reaction, especially from a mainstream media that usually takes the pro-choice side, could be summed up in one sentence: *What was all the fuss about?*

The Focus ad ran in the first quarter and started with Pam, dressed in a simple black outfit, standing against a white background. Above pleasing guitar chords, she spoke in an appealing, warm manner—like she entered your living room with a cup of primrose tea in her hand.

Pam: I call him my miracle baby. He almost didn't make it into this world. I can remember so many times when I almost lost him. It was so hard. Well, he's all grown up now, and I still worry about his health. You know, with all our family's been through, you have to be tough.

Suddenly Tim plows in from stage left and tackles his mom to the floor. But she pops up, hair barely mussed, and addresses her son with a coy scold in her voice:

Pam: Timmy! I'm trying to tell our story here.

Tim: Sorry about that, Mom. You still worry about me, Mom?

Pam: Well, yeah. You're not nearly as tough as I am.

The ad closes with text telling viewers to visit the Focus on the Family Web site, where the interview between the Tebow parents and Jim Daly was posted.

"No mention of abortion, no recounting of the dramatic story," wrote *Politics Daily* columnist David Gibson. "No need. Without any frame of reference, the spot could have been a pitch for osteoporosis medication or the need for universal health care or a reminder not to forget Mother's Day. But everyone knew what the ad was about and the ad didn't have to say anything directly, which is the definition of the perfect advocacy ad. It was charming and disarming and went with the flow of the Super Bowl mania."

Jim Daly said afterward that the CBS network would not permit the word *abortion* to be mentioned anyway, so Focus on the Family had to play by CBS' rules. The main goal of the ad was to drive viewers to the Focus Web site, where they could view Bob and Pam's interview and learn more about the resources available at Focus on the Family. More than 1.5 million people viewed the Tebow interview online. Who knows how many reconsidered their view of abortion?

It remains to be seen if Tim will have to pay a personal cost for appearing in the ad. At a speech held at Lipscomb University in Nashville a couple of months after the Super Bowl, Tim told the college audience that multiple companies informed him they couldn't use him as a spokesman if he went ahead with the Super Bowl ad. That was a small price to pay, Tim said, to spread his message about family and faith.

The D1 coaches worked Tim hard: two hours in the weight room, two hours on the field doing speed work, two hours on quarterback-specific drills, and two hours watching film and studying NFL terminology. Capturing it all was Chase Heavener and his film crew, and the D1 staff downloaded their super slow motion footage into their computers and used the film to show Tim how he could improve his five-step drop, seven-step drop, and throwing motion.

After spending a week in Cool Springs working on his fundamentals, Tim flew to Mobile, where a hungry press corps was chasing the Tim-isn't-ready-for-prime-time angle. "I look at myself as a pretty self-motivated person, so I don't really need to listen to all the critics," Tim told reporters before the Senior Bowl. "But if I need a little extra motivation, they're all there. Maybe just throw them on the top to get a little extra motivation."

Sam and Colt were still mending their throwing shoulders, so they didn't come to Mobile. Tim, meanwhile, wasn't 100 percent either: he was battling strep throat, a 103-degree temperature, and a skeptical football media that smelled blood in the water.

When the Senior Bowl was over, Tim can be excused for wishing he'd never played in Mobile. What a dreary late afternoon for No. 15: two fumbles (one lost), four yards rushing on four attempts, and 50 yards passing on 12 attempts (although he did complete eight throws). Granted, he didn't play much, taking just 23 snaps as he shared playing time with two other quarterbacks on the South squad: West Virginia's Jarrett Brown and Oklahoma State's Zac Robinson. But his critics were waiting with long knives.

"It's simple," said one NFL scout. "He's just not a very good quarterback prospect." Scouts Inc. gave Tim a D+ grade, noting that he "put all his weaknesses on display in a setting that did nothing but magnify them." Todd McShay, one of ESPN's NFL draft gurus, was more muted, declaring that Tim "is just not comfortable as a pro-style quarterback."

Only one voice wasn't pessimistic—the one belonging to a feeling-under-the-weather quarterback from Florida. Tim said he improved every day in practice and that his decision to play in the Senior Bowl was proof of his willingness to work hard on his fundamentals. Yet his subpar performance was enough for many NFL coaches and GMs to sell their stock in Tebow, Inc.—despite Tim's 66 percent college career passing percentage, the dozens of passing records he had set in high school and college, and his unworldly 88–16 touchdown-to-interception ratio as a Gator quarterback.

The fact that Tim had been a winner while playing a hybrid style of running back/passing quarterback—where he punished defenses with his left shoulder as well as with his left arm—didn't count for much in the minds of NFL brass or the draft experts.

COMBINE TIME
Tim returned to Cool Springs to continue working to get rid of his swooping windup so he could pass the ball more quickly.

Was he overhauling his throwing motion? Not really, he said.

"It's more of a tweak," Tim told the press. "It's not necessarily changing my whole motion, just the way I'm holding the ball and kind of how I'm getting to where I'm throwing it. That's kind of the biggest problem we've seen, so that's what we're working on the most."

Tim practiced over and over holding the football higher—at shoulder height—after he received the snap. That movement effectively cut the loop from his throwing motion.

B-roll from Chase Heavener's film crew was released to ESPN and other media outlets showing Tim—under the gaze of his D1 coaches—dropping back seven steps with his left arm cocked high before delivering a tightly thrown pass. Even casual fans could tell his throwing motion was more compact and that he was "getting" to his releases quicker.

Between working on this throwing motion and hopping on private planes to make appearances at the Super Bowl, the Daytona 500, and the National Prayer Breakfast in Washington, D.C., Tim worked insanely hard during the month of February.

Kurt Hester, the corporate director of training at D1, said Tim's work ethic was a problem—"he just goes all-out all the time." Working around all the out-of-state appearances had been tough, Hester said, "but he won't quit. If I told him to get here at three in the morning, he'd get here at three in the morning."

Coming up during the first week of March was the National Invitational Camp, otherwise known as the NFL Combine, which was named after three scouting camps that "combined" or merged in 1985. More than 600 NFL personnel, including head coaches, general managers, and scouts, converged on Indianapolis for the camp.

The 329 players who expected to be drafted were invited to Lucas Oil Field to be weighed and measured and to participate in six measurable drills—40-yard dash, 225-pound bench press repetitions, vertical jump, broad jump, three-cone drill, and shuttle run—as well as individual drills. There would also be psychological evaluations and an IQ exam known as the Wonderlic Test administered.

The process can be dehumanizing; some call the NFL Combine the "Underwear Olympics" and compare the physicals to being poked and prodded like steers on a hoof. The extensive medical exams, which could last up to eight hours, had players clad only in undershorts, standing in a room full of NFL team doctors and scouts as they were weighed, measured, and subjected to a battery of tests—MRIs, EKGs, CT scans, X-rays, and more.

"You're investing a lot of money in some of these guys," said John Spanos, the San Diego Chargers' director of college scouting. "You really want to make sure you're not buying damaged goods."

Aspiring NFL players dare not skip the Combine, and Sam, Colt, and Tim all flew to Indianapolis to participate, even though none of the Three QBs said they would participate in individual throwing drills. All three said they would instead wait until their pro day at their respective alma maters to put their arms to the test in front of NFL evaluators.

Pro days are held at each university under conditions thought to be more favorable for the players. At their pro days, quarterbacks participate in passing drills, and position players run the 40-yard dash, make a vertical jump, do the three-cone drill, and undergo other physical tests in front of an array of NFL coaches and scouts.

The NFL Combine—an entirely different bird—is a four-day process that begins with a preliminary medical examination and orientation. During their first night in Indianapolis, Sam, Colt, and Tim went through a process called "speed dating"—where representatives of every NFL team sit at tables inside small rooms and conduct 10- to-15-minute interviews with each of the players.

"You get dizzy from it all," Sam said just before 11 P.M. after his night of speed dating. "You go from 5:30 in the morning until 11 every night, every day. You better be in good shape when you come here."

If a prospect isn't in good shape physically, the NFL has a way of finding out. The second day is reserved for four extensive medical exams—eight doctors at a time, one from each of the 32 NFL teams. If players, especially quarterbacks, had fudged on their height and weight, it was now out in the open.

Here's how the Three QBs measured up:

- Sam Bradford: 6-4¼, 236 pounds
- Colt McCoy: 6-1⅛, 216 pounds
- Tim Tebow: 6-2¾, 236 pounds

Everyone knew Sam was 6-4 and change, and Tim was usually listed at 6-3, so he wasn't too far off the mark. But Colt's height, which barely topped 6-1, was a red flag to some NFL teams because the typical pro quarterback stands at least 6-2. "I'd like to say I was six-foot-four," Colt said at the Combine, "but this is what God gave me . . . and I'm going to use it as best as I can."

When Colt was asked about being likened to Super Bowl MVP Drew Brees, who stands an even six feet tall, the Texas QB ran with the comparison. "I hope you guys can see that [comparison] because I see it," he said.

Colt participated in only two of the measurable drills— the 40-yard dash and the broad jump. He ran the fifth-fastest time in the 40 among quarterbacks with a 4.79, just behind

Tim's time of 4.72. Sam did not run the 40 or participate in any of the drills.

For quarterbacks, the 40-yard dash ranks far down on the list of priorities; height, arm strength, quick release, escapability, leadership skills, and football knowledge are what matter to the NFL. Ditto for the standing broad jump, a drill where Colt excelled, vaulting nine feet, six inches, but Tim just beat him out, clearing nine feet, seven inches. Tim also wowed the scouts with his 38.5-inch vertical leap, which tied him for the Combine's all-time record for quarterbacks (held by Josh McCown). By way of comparison, Tim's leap was a half-inch higher than Michael Vick's in 2001.

One test the Three QBs—or anyone else at the Combine—couldn't avoid was the Wonderlic, an exam that measures an individual's learning and problem-solving abilities. The Wonderlic Test is made up of 50 not-too-difficult SAT-like questions. The number you answer correctly in 12 minutes is your score; you can't spend more than 15 seconds on each question if you expect to finish.

The average Wonderlic score for NFL quarterbacks is 24, and Sam performed impressively, scoring a 36. Colt posted a 25, but Tim didn't do as well, scoring a 22.

It's difficult to argue that the Wonderlic Test is an accurate determiner of future success for NFL quarterbacks. San Francisco's Alex Smith and Arizona's Matt Leinart scored 40 and 35, respectively, but they haven't exactly lit it up as pros—at least not yet. Hall of Famers Dan Marino and Jim Kelly, however, both scored 15s, and Brett Favre scored a 22, the same as Tim.

SO HOW WOULD YOU SCORE ON THE WONDERLIC TEST?

The clock is ticking . . . and you have just 15 seconds to answer each question. Here are some sample questions from the Wonderlic Test:

1. Look at the row of numbers below. What number should come next?

8 4 2 1 ½ ¼

2. Paper sells for 21 cents per pad. What will four pads cost?

3. The ninth month of the year is:
a. October
b. January
c. June
d. September
e. May

4. Assume the first two statements are true. Is the final one true, false, or not certain?

Tom greeted Beth. Beth greeted Dawn. Tom did not greet Dawn.

5. A boy is 17 years old and his sister is twice as old. When the boy is 23 years old, what will be the age of his sister?

Answers:
1. 1/8
2. 84 cents
3. September
4. not certain
5. 40 years old

Aside from the written exams, Tim also completed five of the six measurable drills, passing on the 225-pound bench press repetitions so he could protect his throwing arm.

There was one individual drill Tim performed at the NFL Combine, however, where you could say his time was a revelation: in the three-cone speed drill, Tim ran a hell-blazing 6.66 seconds, which showed he was a real speed demon.

PRO DAYS AHEAD

With so much at stake—draft position, which team would pick them, and millions of dollars—quarterbacks aspiring to an NFL career leave little to chance. Very few throw at the NFL Combine because they will be passing to unfamiliar receivers at an unfamiliar venue. NFL coaches can also dictate which passing drills they would like to see at the Combine.

As they say at golf's biggest tournaments, you can't win a major on the first day, but you sure can lose it with a poor outing.

Each of the Three QBs had excellent reasons for declining to throw at the Combine. Sam and Colt were coming off shoulder injuries—remember, Sam had missed most of the 2009 college season after undergoing ligament repair surgery, and Colt had suffered a pinched nerve in his shoulder after being rammed to the Rose Bowl turf at the national championship game.

Tim was into his second month of working to get rid of his below-the-belt throwing motion and to perfect the above-the-shoulder delivery NFL coaches like to see in their quarterbacks. The more time he had to practice and improve his new technique, the better chance he had to impress coaches and scouts when it came time to throw at his pro day.

Tim was first to fire up for pro day, and as you would expect, the March 17 event at the University of Florida was a circus. "For all the television time, Internet bandwidth, and newsprint used to discuss Tim Tebow's new throwing motion, anything short of the southpaw walking onto Florida Field and throwing right-handed was found to be a bitter disappointment," wrote *Sports Illustrated*'s Andy Staples.

More than 3,000 spectators and 100 NFL personnel were on hand at The Swamp, including five head coaches and a couple of general managers. Tim wasn't the only Gator athlete under the microscope; teammates Carlos Dunlap, Joe Haden, Aaron Hernandez, and Maurkice Pouncey—all potential first-rounders—were going through their pro day paces as well.

Tim threw for 45 minutes—outs, curls, hitches, posts, comebacks, and gos. He cocked the ball closer to his ear, released the ball much more quickly, and delivered tight spirals where they needed to be. He hit receiver David Nelson on a 45-yard post pattern—in stride. Next throw, the same 45-yard post but to the opposite side of the field, where the deep pass landed in Riley Cooper's arms in full gait.

Tim looked flat-out impressive. The backpedaling on his seven-step drops was an athletic work of art, his command of the field was sure, and his passing was on the money. The debut of his new throwing motion went off without a hitch.

Like the opening of a hit show on Broadway, Tim's new act drew raves. The consensus in the media was that he had shown "ridiculous" improvement. In less than an hour on his favorite field, Tim successfully pushed back a tide of coaching opinion that had threatened to sink his chances of ever playing quarterback in the NFL. He was once again a viable NFL quarterback prospect.

Between pro day and NFL draft day, held five weeks later, Tim scheduled private workouts with several NFL teams, including Seattle, Washington, and New England.

Tim also hoped to get a closer look from the Denver Broncos. During one of the "speed dates" at the NFL Combine, he had sat in a meeting room just a few feet apart from Josh McDaniels, the boyish-looking 33-year-old head coach of the Broncos. They were talking football, and the energy level rose as their eyes locked and their ideas spilled forth. In a word, they *clicked*.

The 15 minutes passed by way too quickly. Tim felt jacked as he left the room. He had met someone with the same passion for football that he had himself. Coach McDaniels was just as intense, just as juiced about finding a way to win in the NFL. He understood where Tim was coming from.

Tim stood up and shook hands with the Broncos coach, and he left the meeting not wanting to visit with another team.

SHOULDERS ARE OKAY

Because they had suffered injuries during their final seasons in college, Sam Bradford and Colt McCoy both had to submit to magnetic resonance imaging (MRI) exams on their right shoulders. No NFL general manager wanted to buy a pig in a poke, and both QBs both knew they'd have to prove their previously injured shoulders were sound.

Their MRIs checked out fine; NFL medical personnel

found nothing else wrong with their shoulders. Sam's repaired shoulder ligaments were as good as new, and Colt's nerve injury had healed just fine. Those in Sam's and Colt's camps breathed easier.

The rehabilitation process hadn't been easy for either player. Following the loss to Alabama at the Rose Bowl, Colt flew to Birmingham, Alabama, to meet with Dr. James Andrews, who told him he didn't need surgery and that he should be as good as new following rehab. Colt then returned to Southern California—after asking Rachel Glandorf to marry him and presenting her with a ring he had designed—and devoted nearly a month to getting his shoulder back in shape.

The road back had been longer for Sam. A few weeks after the skilled hands of Dr. Andrews surgically repaired his shoulder with an absorbable synthetic braid, Sam embarked on a nine-week rehabilitation program at the affiliated Andrews Institute for Orthopaedics and Sports Medicine in Gulf Breeze, Florida. Located on the same campus was Athletes' Performance, Inc., perhaps the premiere training program for elite athletes. The NFL's previous four No. 1 draft picks (Matthew Stafford, 2009; Jake Long, 2008; JaMarcus Russell, 2007; and Mario Williams, 2006) had trained with Athletes' Performance before their NFL Combine and pro day workouts.

Still, the question remained: would Sam be the fifth straight No. 1 pick?

No one was sure, and his situation was dicey in many ways. He had no idea if he'd be able to throw over mountains again. When Sam moved to the Pensacola area of the Florida panhandle to train with Athletes' Performance, he lived alone for the first time in his life and set his nose toward getting back in shape. To combat homesickness, he sent text messages to his family and friends.

Terry Shea, a former college and NFL coach, oversaw Sam's workout program. The first order of business was his footwork. Sam's coaches at Oklahoma had taught him that poor footwork led to poor throws, so he knew it was paramount to set the right foundation before he threw the ball. Also, poor footwork following shoulder surgery could put even more pressure on Sam's tender shoulder, so Shea and Sam worked day after day on tedious footwork drills.

He wouldn't throw a ball for three months.

The 10-hour days in Florida included *beaucoup* hours in the gym—band exercises, BOSU ball, weight training, and free weights. He worked his derriere off, and as his shoulder strengthened, he gradually added more weight plates.

Sam started throwing in late January, keeping things short and easy before progressing to 30-yard throws. The magic in his arm was still there. "They were ropes," Sam said.

Sam grew stronger—and heavier. The time well spent in the weight room had added 13 precious pounds of muscle to his 6 foot, 4¼-inch frame. He hoped the extra weight would help him withstand the poundings of an NFL pass rush.

NFL evaluators at the Combine immediately noticed that Sam had gained muscle mass in his upper body, and the confidence and ease he displayed during his one-on-one meetings in Indianapolis also left a strong impression. His Wonderlic Test results were head and shoulders above his quarterback competition.

A low rumble came out of the Combine and would build

into a roar: Sam Bradford was the guy who would go No. 1 to the St. Louis Rams. The only thing standing in his way was his performance at the pro day at the University of Oklahoma on March 29.

At Sam's pro day, dozens of expressionless football men ringed the sidelines of the Everest Training Center, the Oklahoma football team's indoor training facility. At least 21 NFL teams were represented, and the St. Louis Rams sent four members to observe Sam.

Kent Bradford watched his son complete 13 stationary warm-up passes before Sam threw to moving receivers. Dad kept glancing sideways at the poker-faced NFL coaches and front office personnel, each of them wearing a frozen expression, and he wondered what they were thinking.

Sam began a 50-pass "script" to five different receivers, utilizing a variety of three-step, five-step, and seven-step drops and rollouts. His full virtuosity was on display—from dump-down screens and 10-yard stick routes to a 65-yard bomb that nearly hit the rafters before settling into the arms of his receiver. His teammates and workout partners whooped it up, while the NFL folks murmured (they don't clap at pro days).

After Sam had finished his 49-of-50 workout—there was one drop—Seattle Seahawks coach Pete Carroll tapped out a tweet on his Twitter account: "He lit it up."

NFL überscout Gil Brandt said Sam's workout "almost left me speechless" and was the best workout he'd seen since he watched Troy Aikman, a future Dallas Cowboy quarterbacking great, back in 1988. He had another effusive description for Sam's 30-minute throwing session: "It was a Picasso out there."

The gelling consensus was that Sam's pro day performance had sewn up his spot as the No. 1 pick in the NFL draft. A little more than a week later, the Rams telegraphed their intentions when they released veteran quarterback Marc Bulger . . . on his 33rd birthday.

Bulger, who had played nine seasons for the Rams, saw the handwriting—SAM's COMING!—on the wall, and he asked St. Louis to let him go so he could hook up with a team looking for a backup quarterback.

Some birthday present.

55 FOR 55

Two days after Sam Bradford's brilliant workout, many of the same NFL executives ringed the sidelines of "The Bubble"—the University of Texas indoor practice facility—to watch Colt go through his pro day paces.

Like Sam, a calm and focused Colt threw with something to prove: that he belonged in the same discussion with Sam, Tim, and Notre Dame's Jimmy Clausen. If they were first-round material, then he was, too.

According to Texas offensive coordinator Greg Davis, who scripted the workout, Colt threw 55 passes. Only two were slightly off the mark; his old roommate Jordan Shipley made a diving catch on one ball to save Colt's perfect 55-for-55 performance.

Colt showed off his healed shoulder and excellent form. His eagerness showed in his quick movement and quick strikes. Green Bay Packers coach Mike McCarthy came away suitably impressed, saying Colt's workout was even better than Sam's.

"I like this workout better . . . I thought Colt was challenged more in his workout as far as the type of throws," McCarthy said.

Colt said his favorite throw was off a play-action when he went deep to hit Jordan for 50 yards. He also thought he proved his arm strength with wide-field comebacks and digs to the weak side.

"They wanted to see my footwork underneath center," Colt said afterward. "They [the scouts] told me it was excellent. They wanted to see some play-action, and I felt like I did great at that. They wanted to see my accuracy, and my quick release and what I did on the deep ball. When you go 100 percent, there's really not much you do wrong. I felt like today was really good."

Colt said he enjoyed his "pitch and catch" with Jordan and former Texas receivers Quan Cosby, who was playing for the Cincinnati Bengals, and Nate Jones.

"I can't wait to see where I end up," Colt said.

Without a doubt, the other two QBs were saying the same thing.

5

THE 2010 NFL DRAFT

It used to be that character didn't count for much in the National Football League.

As long as you could deliver blistering hits in the open field, create a hole in the line, make a catch in traffic, or run the two-minute offense, you pretty much got a free pass.

Back in the day, fans were amused by the antics of Broadway Joe Namath—he of the white llama rugs and "bachelor pad" fame who entitled a chapter in his 1970 autobiography "I Like My Girls Blonde and My Johnny Walker Red."

Those relatively innocent days are as long gone as love beads and incense sticks.

Between January 2000 and the spring of 2010, arrests, citations, and drunk-driving charges involving NFL players piled up—495 according to an investigative article in the *San Diego Union-Tribune*. It seems like there's a report every week about an NFL player arrested for public intoxication, driving under the influence, brandishing a weapon, battering a girlfriend, getting caught in a bar fight, or being charged with sexual assault.

One of the most scandalous affairs was an alleged sex party early in the 2005 season involving hookers and 17 Minnesota Viking football players—including the team's starting quarterback—aboard a pair of chartered boats on Lake Minnetonka.

The latest example has been the disturbing revelations about Pittsburgh Steelers quarterback Ben Roethlisberger, accused of sexual assault by a 20-year-old college student who claimed the Steelers QB forced himself upon her in a bar restroom. Although Roethlisberger wasn't formally charged with a crime due to a lack of evidence, NFL Commissioner Roger Goodell handed "Big Ben" a six-game suspension—with the possibility of a reduction to four games—to start the 2010 season.

For years, some NFL teams have closed one eye to character issues in their evaluation of draft prospects. The St. Louis Rams drafted running back Lawrence Phillips in 1996 despite the fact that he received a six-game suspension during his senior year at the University of Nebraska for dragging his girlfriend by her hair down a flight of stairs. The Rams believed the on-the-field reward of playing Phillips in the backfield outweighed any off-the-field risk. Bad call. Phillips was arrested three times in two seasons before the Rams released him . . . for insubordination.

When quarterbacks Peyton Manning and Ryan Leaf were in the running to be selected first in the 1998 NFL draft, Indianapolis Colts president Bill Polian made appointments to meet with both at the NFL Combine. Manning showed up on time, groomed and mature, while Leaf blew off the appointment.

Small actions make big impressions, and the Colts took Manning as the No. 1 pick. The Chargers followed with Ryan Leaf, who quickly unimpressed his teammates and coaches with a lousy work ethic, surly attitude, and profane outbursts at members of the media. Leaf was one of the more remarkable flameouts in NFL history, and many point to his character, or lack of it, as the main reason why.

Then came a disturbing period between April 2006 and April 2007, when the NFL realized it had a serious problem with players of poor conduct and character. At least 79 incidents, including a series of high-profile arrests involving Tennessee Titans cornerback Adam "Pacman" Jones and Cincinnati Bengals wide receiver Chris Henry, prompted Commissioner Goodell to decree a tough personal conduct policy.

When it seemed like NFL rookies stood a better chance of making the police blotter than making the team that drafted them, Goodell and the league had to look at a different way of doing things. The commissioner's personal conduct policy spurred NFL front office personnel to rethink the criteria they used when looking at a professional football player.

THREE "CHARACTER GUYS"

In recent years, the new buzzword in NFL draft war rooms—thank goodness—has been *character*. These days, you're apt to hear GMs say, "He's a character guy," for someone on their draft board, or "He had character issues" for a player they passed on.

Character is one of those intangibles that may be hard to define but is easy to recognize. As someone once pointed out, character means having the inward motivation to do what's right even when nobody is looking. Character means practicing self-restraint regardless of the circumstances. In light of that, it might be a good idea for every football player to memorize this observation from nineteenth-century American newspaper editor Horace Greeley: "Fame is a vapor, popularity an accident, riches take wing, but only character endures."

Going into the 2010 NFL draft, coaches and team personnel were paying attention to character more than ever in making their player evaluations. That's part of why many teams thought so highly of Sam, Colt, and Tim. While there were internal debates about Sam's right shoulder, Colt's height, or Tim's throwing motion, there was a league-wide consensus that the Three QBs were "character guys"—upstanding young men with a strong moral compass.

When the 2010 NFL draft arrived, it turned out that character played a huge role for Sam, Colt, and Tim. Their attitude, work ethic, disposition, and respect for authority were the determining factors in where the Three QBs landed during the draft.

And character issues apparently sank the hopes of another highly touted quarterback.

SAM'S DRAFT DAY

The evolution of the NFL draft from a modest gathering of team officials in smoke-filled rooms at a downtown hotel into a prime-time, made-for-ESPN extravaganza mirrors the growth of football into America's most popular game.

The inaugural NFL draft was held in 1936 at Philadelphia's Ritz-Carlton Hotel and consisted of nine rounds—one for each team in professional football at the time. The number of rounds later ballooned to 30 before receding to today's seven rounds. The doormat of the 1935 NFL football season, the Philadelphia Eagles, chose swivel-hips running back Jay Berwanger from the University of Chicago as their No. 1 pick.

Berwanger was in the news because he had just won the first-ever Downtown Athletic Club Trophy as the most outstanding college football player. The award would be renamed the following year after John Heisman, a trailblazing, turn-of-the-century coach who pioneered the forward pass and originated the use of the word *hike* to start plays. Heisman was also chairman of the Downtown Athletic Club.

The Eagles offered Berwanger $150 a game, a good salary in those Depression-era days. When Berwanger declined, the Eagles traded him to the Chicago Bears—"hometown boy coming back to the Windy City" was how they billed it. When Bears head coach and owner George Halas asked him what he wanted, Berwanger said the figure he had in mind was $25,000 for a two-year contract. Otherwise, he'd put his college education to better use.

Papa Bear Halas smiled and extended his hand, then told Berwanger the Bears couldn't afford such an astronomical amount. Halas wished him the best, and the running back walked away from professional football and never played a down. Berwanger became a foam-rubber salesman and gave the first Heisman Trophy to his aunt Gussie, who used the

25-pound bronze statue as a doorstop in her home.

It's doubtful Sam's Heisman Trophy is being used as a doorstop at the Bradford house these days, just as it's highly improbable that Sam and his agent asked for a two-year contract worth $25,000 following the 2010 NFL draft. Try *two thousand times* that amount—something in the $50 million range, but we're getting ahead of the story here.

After Sam's Picasso-like performance at pro day, when all the doubts regarding his rehabilitated shoulder were put to rest, the die was cast: it was looking more and more like Sam's year to go No. 1.

Holding the top pick were the St. Louis Rams, the worst team in pro football with a 1–15 record in 2009. Drafting Sam wasn't a slam dunk, though; the Rams needed help on both sides of the ball, so they could have traded their No. 1 pick—Sam—for a garden variety of draft picks to help them rebuild a dismal team that had won just six games and lost 42 since 2007.

From the Rams' point of view, there was also the risky business of drafting a quarterback with the No. 1 pick. Since 1970, 17 quarterbacks had gone No. 1. There were booms and busts, but most went on to have so-so careers. The diamonds included Troy Aikman, who went to the Dallas Cowboys and won three Super Bowls for America's Team. Other No. 1-pick quarterbacks who worked out fabulously were Peyton Manning of the Indianapolis Colts, Peyton's brother Eli with the New York Giants, John Elway of the Denver Broncos, Jim Plunkett of the Oakland Raiders, and Terry Bradshaw of the Pittsburgh Steelers—all of whom won Super Bowl rings.

But there were some famous busts like Jeff George and

Tim Couch. JaMarcus Russell, the No. 1 pick in 2007, struggled mightily with the Oakland Raiders, who unceremoniously dumped him following the 2010 NFL draft.

With so much at stake, the Rams would be counted upon to do their due diligence. Head coach Steve Spagnuolo came away impressed with Sam after their 15-minute "speed date" at the NFL Combine. "Everything you hear about him, that's said, it's legit," Spagnuolo said. "He walks into a room, you can see he's a quarterback. That was impressive to me."

Ten Rams officials, including general manager Billy Devaney, were in the crowded Combine meeting room with Sam and Coach Spagnuolo; the room was lit with floodlights because the Rams were taping the interview.

"There were a lot of bodies in there, in kind of a small room," Spagnuolo said. "It was a little intimidating, or it could've been for a 22-year-old guy. And yet, he walked in and did not seem . . . rattled at all."

What Spagnuolo and the Rams were looking for in Sam, besides zip in his arm, were the intangibles—leadership, body language, presence, and how he interacted with coaches. He apparently passed the interview with flying colors.

After the Combine, Devaney and offensive coordinator Pat Shurmur traveled to Florida to meet with Sam at Athletes' Performance, the world-class training facility, and witness for themselves how Sam's rehabilitation was going. They sat down with Sam and talked football, and they also met with Dr. James Andrews, who performed Sam's surgery, to discuss the quarterback's progress in rehab.

Devaney couldn't be blamed for treading cautiously. He was the San Diego Chargers director of player personnel back in 1998 when the Bolts drafted Ryan Leaf, so he knew how first-round picks could turn sour. Although Chargers general manager Bobby Beathard ran the show and made the call on Leaf, Devaney learned a valuable lesson when it came to drafting quarterbacks. Things won't work out "if you don't have the intangibles to play that position," he said. "There's so much that goes into being a quarterback in the NFL. The work ethic you have to have. The leadership. The time that you put in. The media scrutiny. If you can't handle all that stuff, you're going to have a hard time performing on the field."

The 2010 NFL draft would be done a bit differently than in the past. For many years, the draft was a weekend staple, beginning at noon Eastern Time with three rounds on Saturday and finishing up on Sunday. But the 75th draft was the first to kick off in prime time, starting at 7:30 p.m. EST on Thursday, April 22—a move Commissioner Goodell said would make the draft "more accessible to fans." (He obviously wasn't thinking about those on the West Coast who were still at their work cubicles at 4:30 in the afternoon.) ESPN and the NFL Network planned wall-to-wall coverage of the three-day draftapalooza, which would be held at the venerable Radio City Music Hall in Manhattan.

Sam was among the 18 draft prospects invited to New York City for two days of promotion—posing for pictures atop the marquee of Radio City Music Hall, ringing the closing bell at the New York Stock Exchange, and visiting pediatric patients at Kravis Children's Hospital—before hanging out backstage at Radio City Music Hall and waiting for their names to be called—in the first round, they all hoped.

The invitation is quite an honor but can be a two-edged sword because if you're *not* drafted in the first round—or No. 1 when everyone expects you to go as the first pick—your anguish is on full display for the whole world to see from inside the Radio City Music Hall green room.

Sam wasn't sure he wanted to go to New York and step into the hurricane of media attention, but he realized his absence would have cast a shadow over one of pro football's signature events and raised even more questions. "It's a once-in-a-lifetime thing," he said after he arrived in New York the day before the draft. "I figured I didn't want to look back and have any regrets about not going. Everyone said that all the guys who have ever come just really enjoyed their time here, so that's one of the reasons I decided to make the trip."

Nobody expected Sam to wait very long for his name to be called. On the day before the draft, the latest *Sports Illustrated* issue hit the newsstands with Sam on the cover, clad in a crimson Nike Dri-FIT collarless shirt and dark shorts, looking resolute as he dropped back to pass with a football clutched between his hands. CALL TO ARMS: FRANCHISE QBS ARE THERE FOR THE TAKING—AND OKLAHOMA'S SAM BRADFORD TOPS THE LIST was the cover headline.

Would the *Sports Illustrated* cover jinx knock Sam off the No. 1 perch?

Even Sam wasn't sure. Billy Devaney didn't call Sam in advance of the draft to let him know it was a done deal, so the Oklahoma QB was still in the dark at 7:30 p.m. that night when Goodell officially put the St. Louis Rams "on the clock," meaning the club had 10 minutes to either announce its selection or trade the draft choice to another team seeking to "move up."

Four minutes later, Sam's cell phone chirped. Billy Devaney was on the line with the good news: Sam was a Ram—St. Louis' franchise quarterback—and would be forever known as an NFL No. 1 draft pick. The news was relayed to Commissioner Goodell, who strode to the podium:

With the first pick in the 2010 NFL Draft, the St. Louis Rams select Sam Bradford, quarterback, Oklahoma . . .

Watching on a monitor backstage, a relieved Sam gave his father, Kent, a soul shake and a hug, then embraced his mother, Martha, before gamboling to the stage and posing for pictures with the commissioner while wearing a Rams cap and holding a Rams No.1 jersey.

In a conference call with St. Louis reporters a few minutes after his selection, a getting-giddier-by-the-minute Sam talked about the Rams selecting him as the No. 1 pick. "You have no idea how excited I am, just to have the opportunity to come to St. Louis and start my NFL career," he said. "It's just a blessing, and I can't wait to get there and get to work."

"We didn't see any negatives," Devaney said in his remarks afterward. "Rare size. Accuracy off the charts . . . He's a much better athlete than I'd given him credit for early on in this process. Extremely intelligent. Character. I think he's a classy kid. All those things. I happen to think he's the whole package."

So did a lot of people who'd known Sam for a long time.

TIM TEBOW: THE FIRST-ROUND SHOCKER

Tim Tebow was in New York City, too, but not for the NFL draft. He traveled to Manhattan a couple of days earlier to promote *NCAA Football 11*, EA Sports' new college football video game. After making an appearance at an upscale restaurant on lower Broadway and playing his brother Robby in the football video game—Tim was Virginia Tech and Robby was Florida—Tim announced he would be flying back to Jacksonville to accompany his family for the draft, even though he was one of the 18 players the NFL had invited to be in attendance.

"It would have been exciting to be here, to hold your jersey up with the commissioner. That's always something every athlete wants to do," Tim told NFL Network's Charles Davis the day before the draft. "But it's going to be special being at home. Being with my family, my friends, my best friends, my high school teammates, people like that that I know couldn't make their way up here, that I wanted to be able to spend this moment with. That's what it's truly about for me."

The prospect of sitting in the Radio City Music Hall green room—with TV cameras recording every nose twitch—until his name was called understandably lacked appeal in the Tebow camp. Who wants to squirm on national TV as the pressure mounts when you're passed over?

Tim and his parents had no idea whether Tim would be picked in the first round or drop ingloriously to the second, third, or—gasp!—fourth round. From the going-out-on-top Sugar Bowl victory to the Senior Bowl washout to the raves he received for his revamped throwing motion at pro day, Tim's stock among NFL teams fluctuated like the Dow Jones average.

Throughout the spring of 2010—swirling through March Madness, the first pitch of the Major League Baseball season, and Tiger's return to golf—one of the biggest stories in sports remained: *Where will Tim Tebow be drafted?* If an NFL player or coach wanted to get some face time with the media, all he had to do was venture an opinion on Tim's draft day prospects.

Tim's former teammate at Florida, Cincinnati Bengals wide receiver Andre Caldwell, said the right spot to draft the Gator quarterback would be "late second round," adding that the former Heisman winner would need significant time to adjust to life in the NFL. Following Tim's pro day, Miami Dolphins quarterback Chad Henne bluntly told WQAM radio in Miami, "My judgment is that he's not an NFL quarterback. I'll leave it at that."

That's precisely what draftnik Mel Kiper Jr. had been saying since the end of Tim's junior year, when he began ringing the town bell and proclaiming that Tim wasn't NFL quarterback material—and would be better suited to playing professional football as a tight end or H-back. The helmet-haired analyst dissed everything about Tim's quarterbacking skills.

To his credit, Tim did an interview on ESPN Radio with host Freddie Coleman and Kiper at the end of his junior season. The Florida quarterback showed he could think on his feet just as quickly as he could move them after a snap count. "You tell me this," Tim said during his radio exchange with Kiper. "What do you think I need to do to be an NFL quarterback? You tell me that."

Kiper backpedaled like an All-Pro cornerback and mumbled something about the NFL being a "flip of the coin" and that Peyton Manning had his detractors when he came into the league. Said Kiper, "You're too good with the ball in your hands not to think, *Could he be Frank Wycheck? Could he be*

Chris Cooley? That's why," Kiper said. "You're too good, doing what you do, Tim, running with the football."

Wycheck and Cooley were NFL tight ends, but in this context, the comment was a thinly veiled insult since Tim's peers were quarterbacks like Sam and Colt, not journeymen tight ends.

After hearing Kiper out, the Florida quarterback replied, "The quarterback has the ball in his hands every play."

Touché, Tim . . .

In the weeks leading up to the 2010 NFL draft, Tim's name was nowhere to be found on Kiper's "Big Board" of Top 25 picks, but "he's the story of the draft, like him or not," said Peter King of *Sports Illustrated*. For every Tebow doubter, though, there was a Tebow booster. Perhaps the biggest voice in his corner was former Tampa Bay coach Jon Gruden, who had worked out Tim as part of *Gruden's QB Camp* specials that ran on ESPN leading up to draft day. Gruden told anyone who would listen that Tim could very well crack the first round.

"If you want Tim to be on your football team, if you want him bad enough, you're going to have him in the first round or the second," Gruden said. "If you want Tim in your locker room, on your football team, and you can see a little down the road, a team like that is going to take him earlier than some people expect. I'm very confident in this guy."

Preceding the draft, five NFL teams requested private individual workouts with Tim. They were as follows:

- The New England Patriots, whose coach, Bill Belichick, loved the way Tim played and loved that his good friend, Urban Meyer, had coached him. The thinking in Beantown was that All-Universe QB Tom Brady could mentor Tim or that a creative football mind like Belichick could find a spot role for Tim as a tight end/H-back.

- The Seattle Seahawks, whose new coach, former USC head man Pete Carroll, was rebuilding a team with 34-year-old veteran Matt Hasselbeck under center. Carroll's interest in Tim cooled considerably, though, after he traded Seattle's second-round draft pick and cash to San Diego for third-string quarterback Charlie Whitehurst in March.

- The Buffalo Bills, whose former quarterback Hall of Famer Jim Kelly was in Tim's corner. The quarterback position in Buffalo had been a revolving door since Kelly retired; the Bills had started nine different QBs during a decade-long playoff drought. "Whether it's Tim Tebow . . . you look for a guy with good character, good leadership ability, and good arm strength," Kelly said.

- The Minnesota Vikings, who might have had an opening at quarterback if Brett Favre didn't return—or if the soon-to-be-41-year-old NFL legend did come back, Tim could learn from one of the best. The Vikings had the 30th pick in the first round, too.

- The Denver Broncos, whose young head coach, Josh McDaniels, was said to be intrigued with Tim, even though the club had recently traded for Cleveland's Brady Quinn, a third-year pro out of Notre Dame. In the week preceding the draft, the Broncos visited and worked out Tim twice in a five-day span.

Several other teams were rumored to have been flirting with the idea of taking Tim, including the Jacksonville Jaguars, who had the No. 10 pick. The thinking was that Jacksonville wasn't selling out its games, and drafting a local hero like Tim would put fannies in the seats. *Tebowmania stays in Florida!* Throughout the spring, though, the Jags hadn't shown the slightest interest in Tim. Was it a head feint? A move not to tip their hand?

Or maybe something really wild would happen—like Pittsburgh trading bad boy Ben Roethlisberger and bringing in Boy Scout Tim Tebow, but that was held to be as unlikely as Mel Kiper getting a Mohawk haircut.

Kiper and his ESPN sidekick, Todd McShay, stuck to their guns regarding Tim's draft prospects. "I think Tim has got to develop into a starting quarterback to be worth being a second-round choice," said Kiper, showing his belief that the first round was beyond the realm of reason for Tebow. "I don't think he can be. Others do. We'll see . . . I'll root for Tim to prove me wrong on that one."

McShay called Tim a "project" and said he'd be surprised if any team parted with a cherished first-round pick for him. "I would not draft Tebow in the first two rounds. My philosophy is you draft people who have a legitimate shot to be starter right away."

Through it all, Tim's faith and confidence never wavered. On the morning of the NFL draft, he told *USA Today*, "I believe I'll be drafted as a quarterback and used as a quarterback."

After the St. Louis Rams tabbed Sam as the No. 1 pick, the NFL draft proceeded down a fairly expected avenue, although the San Diego Chargers gambled by trading up to No. 12 and drafting a much-needed running back, Ryan Mathews of Fresno State, to replace LaDainian Tomlinson.

Two highly regarded Florida Gator teammates were drafted ahead of Tim: the Cleveland Browns took cornerback Joe Haden with the seventh pick, and the Pittsburgh Steelers selected center Maurkice Pouncey—who did a great job protecting Tim at Florida—with the 18th pick. It turned out Ben Roethlisberger wasn't going anywhere after all.

Tim watched the draft unfold at a private residence at Jacksonville's Glen Kernan Country Club, surrounded by two or three dozen family members, close friends, and others in the Tebow camp, including his agent, Jimmy Sexton. Sitting in the corner of the living room was a cardboard box stuffed with Denver Broncos hats.

They knew.

A few—*very* few—put two and two together before the draft. On draft day eve, Mike Klis, a sports columnist for *The Denver Post*, wrote that, yes, he could see the Broncos taking Tim Tebow. The way he envisioned things, the Broncos would trade back their No. 11 pick and get an extra second-round selection, and then offer a team a package of second-round picks to grab Tim somewhere in the first round—between No. 20 and No. 30. Klis then offered these reasons:

1. If Coach McDaniels was bold enough to trade away talented quarterback Jay Cutler and All-Pro receiver Brandon Marshall, then he'd have the steel nerve to draft Tim Tebow.

2. McDaniels liked proven winners with good height standing in the pocket. Tim met both requirements.

3. McDaniels was big on all his players, quarterbacks or otherwise, being men of good character and football smarts.

4. McDaniels' brother, Ben, was the Broncos quarterback coach, and they saw themselves as just the right team to bring Tim along.

5. While Tim developed and watched starting Broncos quarterback Kyle Orton, he could come in for four or five plays a game as a "Wildcat QB" and make those tough third-and-two and fourth-and-one conversions for first downs. *Shades of his freshman year at Florida.*

Mike Klis called it; the Broncos indeed took Tim in the first round. But you need a flow chart to follow the Broncos' crazy route to using the No. 25 pick to select Tim Tebow.

- First, the Broncos traded their No. 11 pick to the San Francisco 49ers for the Niners' first-round pick (No. 13) and a fourth-round pick.

- Next, the Broncos sent the No. 13 pick to Philadelphia in exchange for the Eagles' first-round pick (No. 24) and two third-rounders.

- Then the Broncos traded the No. 24 pick (as well as a fourth-round choice) to New England for the Patriots' first-round pick (No. 22), which they used *not* to draft Tim Tebow but Georgia Tech receiver Demaryius Thomas.

- Three picks later, the Broncos grabbed the No.

25 pick from Baltimore in exchange for the Ravens' second-, third-, and fourth-round picks. The Broncos also received the No. 119 pick in the deal.

All this shuffling momentarily confused the ESPN talking heads. Could it be that Denver . . . ?

And that's when Tim's cell phone rang with a 303 area code.

"Should I answer it?" he asked his agent, Jimmy Sexton.

Of course, Tim.

Coach McDaniels was on the line, but he didn't seem at all in a hurry to get down to business. He made small talk and asked Tim if he was enjoying the night. *Oh, and by the way, we're going to trade up and take you.*

The electrifying news swept through the living room just as an ESPN camera cut away to the joyful scene of Tim hugging his family and friends. Then Team Tebow brought out the Broncos hats, and Tim, wearing an ear-to-ear grin, slipped one on.

At 10:09 P.M., in the midst of the pandemonium, Commissioner Goodell's official announcement came that Tim Tebow was a first-round draft choice of the Denver Broncos. The proclamation sent shock waves through Radio City Music Hall and caused Mel Kiper Jr. to blanche like he'd just swallowed a dose of cod liver oil.

"I just think I showed them [the Broncos] I was willing to do whatever it took," Tim told ESPN. "I want to thank everyone in the organization. Over the last few weeks, we really hit it off. I was hoping and praying that was where I could play."

Tim said his private workout three days earlier with the

Denver coaching staff raised his hopes that Denver would be the team that would take him. "It was awesome," he said of his day in Denver. "It was a day full of ball. We talked ball, watched film. We watched so much stuff . . . . It was the best day I've had. I enjoyed it. Their coaches are awesome. It was great. Their coaches are just likes the coaches I have at Florida. I'm just excited to be a Bronco."

The Denver media reported that the Broncos knocked the NFL on its insignia ears by selecting Tim, and headlines around the country called Denver's drafting of Tim "shocking" and "surprising."

There was electricity in the rarefied Colorado air, but there were also some interesting dynamics regarding the pick. The Centennial State is really the tale of two cities: Denver, the state capital, and Colorado Springs, 60 miles to the south, along the Front Range corridor. Denver (and nearby Boulder) is uniformly more liberal, while Colorado Springs, which is home to dozens of Christian ministries, including Focus on the Family, is more conservative.

Would Tim be a polarizing figure in such an environment?

"Tim Tebow is a lightning rod," said Bill McCartney, the former University of Colorado football coach and founder of the Promise Keepers men's ministry, adding, "There is an anointing on Tim and his family. He's one of those guys who comes along who has God's handprints all over him." McCartney predicted that Tim, who's heavily involved in philanthropic efforts through his Tim Tebow Foundation, would make a difference for Denver's poor and oppressed.

Perhaps that's why *Denver Post* columnist Woody Paige—

a regular panelist on the ESPN sports-talk program *Around the Horn* who is not known for any conservative views— preached tolerance shortly after Tim was drafted. The headline on his sympathetic column: IT's NOT FAIR TO RIP TEBOW FOR HIS FAITH.

Time will tell how the Mile High City receives Tim, but everywhere he's played, he's won over his teammates and fans with his discipline, hard work, uncompromising effort, and legendary work ethic.

That doesn't figure to change now that he's a Denver Bronco.

COLT MCCOY: STAYING IN ORANGE

Colt McCoy wasn't drafted on the first night of the 2010 NFL draft, but then again, he wasn't expected to go in the first round.

Nearly every NFL draftnik with a platform declared that Colt was no better than the fourth-best quarterback in the draft anyway, lodged behind Sam, Tim, and Notre Dame quarterback Jimmy Clausen. For months, Mel Kiper had said that the most "pro-ready quarterback" in the 2010 draft was not Sam or Tim or Colt but Jimmy Clausen.

As was the case with Tim, the NFL didn't believe Kiper's siren call about Clausen, and there was a reason why—those pesky "intangibles."

A couple of NFL scouts, speaking anonymously, told CBS Sports the reason Clausen dropped all the way to the No. 48 pick—23 spots behind Tim—was due to his personality, not his mechanics and capabilities on the field. "With what I was listening to, I thought I was hearing Ryan Leaf all over again," said one scout. "He has a sense and a degree of entitlement that's off the charts." Another scout added, "I heard horror stories about the guy off the field to the point where I wasn't interested."

Jimmy Clausen suffered a precipitous fall in the NFL draft. Colt McCoy did not, even though the Cleveland Browns eventually drafted him with the 85th pick. In fact, Colt wound up with a team that's a great match for his dogged style of playing quarterback—an appropriate metaphor since the Browns' zealous fans, known as the Dawg Pound, take up residence behind the east end zone of Cleveland Browns Stadium.

You see, the reason Colt was picked late in the third round was the NFL's fixation with height and heft. Since Colt was "only" 6-1 and 216 pounds—the measureables—there was concern that his body could not hold up to the pounding he could expect while slinging passes from an NFL pocket. The intangibles, though, were no problem; Colt had checked out as a "character guy." Cleveland Browns first-year president Mike Holmgren—a proven winner in the NFL following coaching stints at Green Bay and Seattle—wanted Colt all along, but on his terms, meaning the third round.

There was some symmetry working. Holmgren had been the quarterbacks coach with the San Francisco 49ers in the 1980s when the West Coast team drafted a relatively unheralded quarterback from Notre Dame—also in the third round. At 6-2 and 205 pounds, Joe Montana wasn't a player of "NFL prototype" size, but he still managed to cobble together a 15-year career that left him with four Super Bowl rings on his fingers and a Hall of Fame career in his back pocket.

Holmgren had brought Colt to Cleveland for a private workout a couple of weeks before the draft. The quarterback hopeful also spent time with Coach Eric Mangini and practiced with Browns quarterbacks Jake Delhomme and Seneca Wallace. Similar to the bond that quickly developed between Denver coach Josh McDaniels and Tim Tebow, Colt felt something click with the Browns' Mike Holmgren. His sure, experienced hand with producing quality quarterbacks felt assuring to Colt.

The Cleveland Browns weren't the only team taking a close look at Colt. Exactly two weeks before draft, he had an hour-long private workout in Austin for the St. Louis Rams in front of Billy Devaney, Steve Spagnuolo, and quarterbacks coach Dick Curl. Devaney said afterward that Colt was extremely impressive and showed "all the stuff that you look for in a great quarterback."

Let the guessing game begin . . . *if the Rams pass on Sam Bradford and draft top defensive tackle Ndamukong Suh instead, they could take Colt in the second round . . . .*

Colt worked out for several other teams, including the New England Patriots and the Washington Redskins. Leading up to the draft, he was like dozens, if not hundreds, of other hopefuls: he had no idea where he'd end up.

Colt and his family, along with his fiancée, Rachel Glandorf, gathered with friends at a spacious Austin home for the first round and returned the following night for rounds two and three. As the second evening played out and his name wasn't called, he spoke with his old coach at Texas, Mack Brown, who was at Radio City Music Hall as a guest commentator for the NFL Network.

"Don't worry, Son, you're in a great place," said his old coach. "You hang in there."

"Coach, I've been through this my whole life," Colt said. "I just want to go to a team that wants me, and I'm going to prove it again."

Then two of the most wonderful omens appeared. The first was the announcement of the No. 84 pick by the Cincinnati Bengals, who selected wide receiver Jordan Shipley, Colt's childhood buddy and teammate from the Texas team.

Then, a minute later, someone new walked to the podium at Radio City Music Hall. It wasn't Commissioner Goodell but Coach Brown holding a card. Fans sitting in the mezzanine took up a chant: "Colt, Colt, Colt . . ."

Wait . . . could it be?

"With the 85th pick in the 2010 NFL draft, the Cleveland Browns select Colt McCoy, quarterback, Texas," announced his old coach.

Back in Austin, Colt hugged his parents, accepted a kiss on the cheek from Rachel, and became a Cleveland Brown.

Mike Holmgren had looked past Colt's measureables, just like Mack Brown had six years earlier when he offered a scholarship to a high school junior from a tiny 2A high school in Tuscola, Texas.

"Nobody expected Colt to have the career that he had at Texas because he came from a small school, and he's a little bit shorter, a little thin—all the things they still say about him," Brown said after the draft. "My expectation is that he'll do a great job in the NFL."

TIM AND THE NATIONAL PRAYER BREAKFAST

Back in early February 2010, shortly after the horrible earthquake that struck Haiti, Tim Tebow was asked to wrap up the National Prayer Breakfast. It's quite an honor to be asked to close such an august event, held annually in Washington, D.C., and attended by the president of the United States, U.S. senators, and members of Congress. Around 3,000 people were on hand for the 2010 gathering, including Vice President Joe Biden and Secretary of State Hillary Clinton.

President Barack Obama, who had addressed the audience earlier, had left by the time Senator Johnny Isakson of Georgia took the podium to introduce Tim. Calling him a "role model for the youth of America," Isakson joked that he found it funny that a fan of University of Georgia football would invite a former member of the Florida Gators to present a closing prayer.

The audience enjoyed a chuckle, and as Tim accepted the microphone, he quipped, "It is rather incredible that a Georgia Bulldog invited a Florida Gator, so you can see the hand of God here."

Tim bowed his head and delivered a wonderful prayer that included the eye black verses worn in the Senior Bowl game:

> Dear Jesus, thank You for this day. Thank You for bringing together so many people that have a platform to influence people for You.
>
> Lord, as we disperse today, let us be united in love, hope, and peace. Lord, let us come together as one and break down all the barriers in between us that separate us. Lord, You came to seek and save that which is lost, and we thank You for that. Lord, we don't know what the future holds, but we know who holds the future, and in that

there is peace, and in that there is comfort, and in that there is hope.

Lord, we pray for the people all over the world who are hurting right now, Lord. The verse that comes to mind is James 1:2–4, "Consider it all joy, my brethren, whenever you encounter various trials, knowing that the testing of your faith produces endurance. And let endurance have its perfect result, that you may be perfect and complete, lacking in nothing."

And we pray for the people in Haiti right now, Lord, that You make them perfect and complete because You love them and have a plan for their lives, just as You do with our lives now.

So my prayer, as we leave today, is that we are united as one because of You. We love You and thank You. In Jesus' name, amen.

MAKING A GAME PLAN

So what will happen to these three special NFL rookies?

Nobody can know that for sure, but that's part of why we can't keep our eyes off these three talented quarterbacks, right? Not knowing what will happen in sports is why we spend our hard-earned money to attend football games or invite a bunch of friends over to watch the Big Game together. Sports—especially American football—have a way of rousing our passions and furnishing us with a bonding experience. Games provide rich experiences, add spice to our weekends, and, when kept in the proper perspective, become part of the tapestry of life.

There will be some great storylines to follow:

• Will "Sam the Savior" turn around a St. Louis Rams

franchise that fell on hard times after another solidly Christian quarterback, Kurt Warner, led them to the "Greatest Show on Turf"—a three-year run at the top that included a Super Bowl victory in 1999?

- Will Colt beat out veterans Jake Delhomme and Seneca Wallace—or get his chance if injury should take either Cleveland quarterback off the field?

- Will Tim write a storybook beginning to his NFL career in Denver by—? You fill in the blank because anything and everything could happen to Tim Tebow. You almost have to laugh at the possibilities, especially when you realize that Tim's first game as a Denver Bronco takes place in his hometown of Jacksonville, against the Jaguars, on Sunday, September 12. And later in the season, on November 28, the Broncos host the St. Louis Rams at Invesco Field, which should give the football pundits something to talk and write about.

So pull up a chair and enjoy what unfolds during Sam's, Colt's, and Tim's rookie seasons in professional football. Be thankful that we have three godly young men seeking to use their physical gifts for the glory of God, but also pray for Sam, Colt, and Tim.

Pray that they will stay close to the Lord and keep their eyes upon Him.

Pray that they will be humble and strong, free from injury, and remain bold witnesses for Christ.

And finally, pray that they will play with purpose.

AFTERWORD

BY TRENT DILFER:
SUPER BOWL-WINNING QUARTERBACK
AND NFL ANALYST FOR ESPN

Author's note: When Fresno State quarterback Trent Dilfer was the sixth player taken in the first round of 1994 draft by the Tampa Bay Buccaneers, expectations ran high that Trent would turn around a franchise that had lost at least 10 games a season for the previous 11 years.

He struggled early on but blossomed in his fourth year with Tampa Bay, putting together a solid season that catapulted the Bucs into the playoffs and earned Trent a Pro Bowl appearance. After six up-and-down seasons with Tampa Bay, though, he signed with the Baltimore Ravens as a free agent to back up highly touted quarterback Tony Banks. Trent accepted that role, but when Banks faltered, Trent got his chance and led the Ravens to 11 straight victories, including a clutch performance in Super Bowl XXXV—ironically played in Tampa—where the Ravens spanked the New York Giants, 34–7.

"Redemption" was the word often associated with Trent's name following the Super Bowl win, but he had experienced

a better kind of redemption when he attended a Fellowship of Christian Athletes camp during his junior year of college and finally understood what it meant to be a Christian. One thing he learned was that following Christ meant paying attention to others, not getting everyone else to pay attention to him.

That focus on Someone greater than him would be what he and his wife, Cassandra, would rely on when they lost their five-year-old son, Trevin, to a heart condition in 2003. Trent's faith sustained him during this trying ordeal, and he said that heaven got a lot more real when he realized that he would have a child waiting for him. One day, they would be reunited.

Trent retired from professional football after the 2007 season and joined ESPN as an NFL analyst for a variety of ESPN programs, including NFL Live, NFL PrimeTime, Monday Night Countdown, *and* SportsCenter. *After playing 14 seasons as an NFL quarterback as well as being recognized for his solid commitment to Christianity—Trent won the Bart Starr Award given to the NFL player who best exemplifies character and leadership—he is just the right person to say a few words to Sam, Colt, and Tim as we close this book.*

As a former NFL quarterback who gets paid to offer his opinions about pro football, I'm really looking forward to the arrival of Sam Bradford, Colt McCoy, and Tim Tebow into the National Football League. This is going to be fun.

I've never met Sam, I have met Tim briefly, and I know Colt pretty well. After Colt's career at Texas ended at the Rose Bowl, he signed with sports agent David Dunn, who happens to be my agent. David asked me if I would help Colt—as well as a couple of other just-out-of-college quarterbacks—get ready for the NFL Combine and upcoming NFL draft in early 2010. I was glad to help out, and I wasn't compensated for my efforts.

At Mission Viejo High School in Southern California's Orange County, I worked with Colt and quarterbacks Sean Canfield and Zac Robinson, giving them my two cents on what they needed to work on to impress NFL scouts. Colt was inquisitive and asked good questions. It was clear that he had high expectations for himself. He wanted to know how he could get better and what he needed to work on. I appreciated that attitude and constantly pushed him to improve his skill set at the quarterback position.

Without getting too technical, I helped Colt refine his throwing motion to make him even more efficient. I'm a big believer that quarterbacks have to be more "compact" in everything they do in the NFL, meaning they have to play in tight spaces. In college, Colt, Sam, and Tim usually threw to open receivers who were easy find because of good separation.

In the pros, however, there is almost *always* tight coverage. They'll have a split second to get the ball in there, and they'll have to learn to throw the ball very accurately into tighter windows as well as make throws from what I call "cluttered quarters." To do that, they'll have to be more compact in their footwork as well as their upper body mechanics.

I told Colt that I thought he used a lot of arm and not enough body to throw the ball, which I identified through film and through watching him in action. He really was only using 60 to 70 percent of his strength when he threw the ball, so that tells me he has a lot more in the tank than he's ever shown. I was just helping him unleash more of his talent when he throws the football, which was something I had to do when I got drafted. I wish I had worked harder on my mechanics earlier in my career.

I haven't worked with Sam or Tim, but if the Three QBs were sitting in my living room, the best advice I would share about entering the NFL is this: *Understand the magnitude of the position.* While many agree with me that the quarterback plays the most important position in sports, I would also argue that playing quarterback is the most *influential* position in all of sports.

Think about it. The way you play and approach the position impacts so many people beyond your immediate sphere of influence—your teammates, your coaches, and your family. The way you play can affect an entire city and even several states, sending shock waves across the country—but the way you play also affects people you never think about. Maybe it's the secretary in the team's front office, the single-parent mom with two kids. If you don't play well and the general manager gets fired, she's going to lose her job, too. That's a small example, but understanding the magnitude of the quarterback position will heighten your awareness and propel you to properly handle your business.

I must also remind you that there are very few things that translate from the college game to the NFL when playing the quarterback position. You will have to relearn a lot of things from a fundamental standpoint, from a technical standpoint, and even from a leadership standpoint with the older athletes—some in their 30s—in your locker room.

You're young rookie players who need to focus on the education of the position and learning what successful quarterbacks do. You'll have to improve. You'll have to do a lot of work to get better while keeping that constant motivation, so think of every day as an opportunity to get better. When I came into the NFL, I thought this was a talent-driven league. It's not. It's a craft-driven league. You have to maximize your talent by honing your craft, and for a quarterback, that means working on your mechanics all the time.

Sam, you're in a unique position as the No. 1 draft pick in the 2010 NFL draft. I would find a big Post-It note and write the following words: *Earn it.* Then I'd stick that note on a mirror in your bedroom or bathroom.

When Peyton Manning signed a seven-year contract worth $98 million in 2004, he was asked at a press conference, "What are you going to do with the money?"

Peyton glared back at the reporter with the same icy determination he displays with a fourth-and-two call. "I'm going to earn it," he announced, adding that is how he has always felt about the money he makes as an athlete.

That's the perspective you need to have as the No. 1 draft pick with a big contract—a constant motivation to earn your salary, earn the respect of your teammates, and earn victories. Keep working at your craft, and keep getting better and better every day. *Earn it.*

Tim, I'll start by saying that I'm rooting for you as much as anybody. You are a unique individual with leadership skills that are God-given and not from man. I know you've been working hard on your fundamentals and focusing on improving your throwing motion. Continue to educate yourself about what successful quarterbacks do and retrain your quarterbacking instincts.

Colt, as I told you in Southern California, it's not how you start but how you finish. Where you got drafted has very few ramifications for your long-term success. I think you went to a great spot with the Cleveland Browns. You'll be developed. You'll be handled properly. You won't be rushed into playing.

Congratulations on your marriage to Rachel in July. I was married my rookie year, so I think it's a good thing. One of the challenges you will have as a young player in this league, and this goes for all three of you, is that you'll be on an emotional roller coaster. It's easy to say that you're not going to listen to all the outside voices, especially from the media and bloggers, but it's hard not to do. Because of that, it's hard to stay on an even keel emotionally.

I think being married and embracing your marriage relationship and trusting Rachel as your best friend will be very helpful because there will be some dark moments. It's comforting to share those dark moments with someone you know intimately, and obviously Rachel is that person for you.

Finally, I know all three of you are aware of this, but I would urge you to get hooked up spiritually with likeminded people. Iron sharpens iron. Growing in your faith is ultimately more important than growing as a player.

Anyone who tells you that growing spiritually will translate into on-the-field success isn't telling you the truth. That's not what the Bible teaches. God doesn't say, *If you follow Me, you're going to be successful on the football field.*

Instead, we're all called to grow in our faith, to mature in God's grace, no matter what our profession or calling is— NFL quarterback, corporate executive, department store cashier, parking lot attendant, student . . . whatever.

Sam, Colt, and Tim, I'm sure you'll do great. I can't wait to watch what unfolds from my chair inside the ESPN studios.

ACKNOWLEDGMENTS

I have to admit I didn't know that much about Sam Bradford, Colt McCoy, and Tim Tebow when I started writing *Playing with Purpose*. That's because I live in San Diego, and while I love college football—during the 2009 season, I witnessed games in South Bend, Indiana (Notre Dame versus Michigan State); Corvallis, Oregon (Oregon State versus Arizona); Berkeley, California (Oregon State versus Cal); and Los Angeles (Oregon State versus USC) *and* the 2010 Rose Bowl (Oregon versus Ohio State)—I think you can understand why I view myself as a Pac-10 guy. After all, I've lived much of my life on the West Coast, graduated from the University of Oregon, and like following the Oregon State Beavers because head coach Mike Riley used to coach my hometown NFL team, the San Diego Chargers. His wife, Dee Riley, is great friends with my wife, Nicole, and we were in a couples' Bible study with the Rileys.

As I began researching and talking to people acquainted with the Three QBs, I quickly realized that those who have known these three young men since their high school and college days had wide grins on their faces. The phrase I kept hearing and reading about each of them was, "He's the real deal." They all know the Three QBs as young men who have "run with perseverance the race marked out for [them]," as Hebrews 12:1–2 says, fixing their eyes on "Jesus, the author and perfecter of [their] faith."

David Wheaton, author of *University of Destruction*, said research shows that 50 percent of young Christians who go to college end up losing their faith—or at least make it a low priority—by the time they graduate. Not so with these three young men. In fact, if anything, they became bolder about proclaiming their faith while they were on their college campuses.

Check out the terrific *I Am Second* videos Sam and Colt have posted on the Internet (just type "I Am Second" into your Web browser); they are very moving and well-produced. Tim Tebow has been standing up before audiences and preaching since he was a teenager, and that boldness carried right through his college career. Don't be surprised if, when his football career is over, Tim begins sharing the gospel message in stadiums, schools, and prisons here in the United States and around the world.

So the first people I want to acknowledge are Kent and Martha Bradford, Brad and Debra McCoy, and Bob and Pam Tebow. Your boys wouldn't be where they are today without your guiding hands, measured discipline, and instillation of godly values.

Well done, good and faithful servants.

The idea for *Playing with Purpose* comes from my literary agent, Greg Johnson of WordServe Literary Group in Denver, Colorado—which is ironic since he now has a front-row seat for Tebowmania in the Rockies. Throughout the winter of 2010, Greg kept pitching to me the idea of writing a book about these three young quarterbacks. I hesitated at first, but then something clicked, and after I put together a proposal, Greg found Barbour Books within a week. My editing team at Barbour, Paul K. Muckley and Tracy M. Sumner, were great to work with. Thanks for the partnership!

Writing this book was like running the two-minute offense without any time-outs—I didn't have much time and the clock was running. Jill Ewert, editor of *Sharing the Victory* magazine, gave me her insights. Kent Bowles and Reagan Lambert of Fellowship for Christian Athletes at Oklahoma and Texas, respectively, pointed me in the right direction. Patina Herrington, whose husband suffered a grand mal seizure and was rescued by Colt, told me their story and read chapters as I finished them.

And finally, I'd like to thank my wife, Nicole, who did tape transcriptions and edited chapters as I wrote them. For someone who grew up in Switzerland and doesn't know an onside kick from a field goal, she did an awfully good job helping me out on a football book.

SOURCE MATERIAL

INTRODUCTION

"The number of traffic tickets issued to Tim Tebow . . . "
"That's the Ticket," *San Diego Union-Tribune*, January 4, 2010, page D2.

"I've interviewed all three players . . . "
Author's interview of *Sharing the Victory* editor Jill Ewert, April 5, 2010.

"People have used the term 'perfect storm' . . . "
Author's interview of Reagan Lambert, April 7, 2010.

"Green Bay Packers quarterback Aaron Rodgers says . . . "
"Hardest, Riskiest, Toughest, Greatest Job in Sports," by Peter King, *Sports Illustrated,* September 7, 2009, available at http://sportsillustrated.cnn.com/vault/article/magazine/MAG1159769/2/index.htm

". . . framed poem on his wall . . ."
"SEC Preview: Florida's Odd Couple Give Gators Bite," by Kelly Whiteside, *USA Today*, August 23, 2007, and available at http://www.usatoday.com/sports/college/football/sec/2007-08-23-florida-oddcouple_N.htm

1. SAM BRADFORD: THE DYNAMITE QUARTERBACK

"Where's Rudy When You Need Him?"
"Bradford's Dad Wants to Avoid Spotlight," by John Helsley,
The Oklahoman, August 22, 2007, and available at
http://www.newsok.com/article/3107688?searched=
%22Kent%20Bradford%22&custom_click=search

"It wasn't even Halloween."
"Sooner (and Cowboy) Born," by John E. Hoover,
Tulsa World, November 28, 2008, and available at
http://www.tulsaworld.com/site/printerfriendlystory.
aspx?articleid=20081128_92_B1_TOPKen88370

". . . show off his ball collection . . . "
"Parents Are Wind Beneath Bradford's Wings," by Jenni
Carlson, *The Oklahoman*, December 12, 2008, and available
at http://www.scrippsnews.com/node/39089

". . . put me on a soccer field today, I would be clueless."
"Q&A with Oklahoma QB Sam Bradford," by Eric Edholm,
ProFootballWeekly.com, April 5, 2010, and available at
http://sports.yahoo.com/nfl/news?slug=pfw-20100406_qa_
with_oklahoma_qb_sam_bradford

"We can't move to Canada. Our lives are in Oklahoma."
"Hockey and the Heisman: Sam Bradford," by Danielle
Bernstein, *USA Hockey* magazine, Issue 3, 2009, and
available at http://www.usahockeymagazine.com/article/
2009-03/hockey-and-heisman-sam-bradford

"I definitely think their attitudes had a great deal of impact . . ."
"Heisman Hopeful Oklahoma Quarterback Sam Bradford Has Been Boosted by the Love and Support of His Parents," by Jenni Carlson, *The Oklahoman*, December 12, 2008, and available at http://newsok.com/the-one-and-only/article/3329566

"Sam's cello ended up in a closet . . ."
"A Different Tune for Bradford," by Thayer Evans, *New York Times*, December 6, 2008, and available at http://thequad.blogs.nytimes.com/tag/sam-bradford/page/2/

"Hockey is so fast and unpredictable . . ."
"Hockey and the Heisman: Sam Bradford," by Danielle Bernstein, *USA Hockey* magazine, Issue 3, 2009, and available at http://www.usahockeymagazine.com/article/2009-03/hockey-and-heisman-sam-bradford

"We were playing sports every weekend, and it's not like I didn't know who God was . . ."
"More Q&As with Bradford and Robinson," by Jenni Carlson, *The Oklahoman*, April 29, 2009, and available at http://blog.newsok.com/jennicarlson/2009/04/29/more-qs-as-with-bradford-and-robinson/

"No Offseason"
"Three-Sport Threat: Sam Bradford," by Andrew Gilman, *The Oklahoman*, March 25, 2005.

"Hanging out with friends, listening to an engaging middle school pastor . . ."
"Sam Bradford's Strategy for Success," by Jonathan Cyprowski and Shawn Brown of *The 700 Club*, and available at http://www.cbn.com/700club/features/amazing/sam_bradford041509.aspx

"Meet Sam Bradford, High School Sophomore Quarterback"
"Sam Bradford, Putnam North," *The Oklahoman,* September 4, 2003, and available at http://www.newsok.com/article/1070234?searched=Sam%20Bradford%2C%20Putnam&custom_click=search

"Sam came in and showed us he was the guy."
Author's interview with Putnam North head football coach Bob Wilson, April 9, 2010.

". . . watched the boy fashion a swing. The ball rose in flight . . . "
"Q&A with Oklahoma QB Sam Bradford," by Eric Edholm, ProFootballWeekly.com, April 5, 2010, and available at http://sports.yahoo.com/nfl/news?slug=pfw-20100406_qa_with_oklahoma_qb_sam_bradford

"Then Long learned something about Sam that sealed the deal . . . "
"Golf Was OU Quarterback Sam Bradford's Special Link," *The Oklahoman*, March 2, 2009.

"If I come here, I'm coming to play . . ."
"Seeking Depth, Oklahoma Got Much More," by Thayer
Evans, *New York Times*, December 6, 2008, and available at
http://www.nytimes.com/2008/12/06/sports/ncaafootball/
06oklahoma.html?_r=1

"According to reports, Bomar had an arrangement . . ."
"Oklahoma Bombshell," by Stewart Mandell, SI.com,
August 2, 2006, and available at http://sportsillustrated.cnn.
com/2006/writers/stewart_mandel/08/02/mandel.bomar/

"Kent Bradford was on cloud nine."
"OU Names Bradford Starting Quarterback," by John E.
Hoover, *Tulsa World*, August 21, 2007, and available at
http://www.tulsaworld.com/sportsextra/OU/article.aspx?su
bjectid=92&articleid=070821_2__Oklah55185&archive=yes

"Sam told CBN's Shawn Brown that his patience and
perseverance . . ."
"Sam Bradford's Strategy for Success," by Jonathan Cyprowski
and Shawn Brown of *The 700 Club,* and available at http://
www.cbn.com/700club/features/amazing/sam_brad-
ford041509.aspx

"Bradford said it's not that he identifies with David, even
though there are similarities."
"Bradford Solves Sooners' Problems with Ease," by Evan
Maisel, ESPN.com, published January 6, 2009, and available at http://sports.espn.go.com/ncf/bowls08/columns/
story?columnist=maisel_ivan&id=3812989

"Coach Wilson was on board . . ."
"Sooners Eyeing the No-Huddle; All the Top Teams in
the Big 12 Are Using It," by Jake Trotter, *The Oklahoman*,
March 17, 2008, and available at http://www.newsok.com/
article/3217125?searched=Sam%20Bradford%2C%20
Bob%20Wilson&custom_click=search

". . . they vaulted themselves to the top of the major college
football polls . . . "
"Sooners No. 1 in Major College Football Polls," by John E.
Hoover, *Tulsa World*, September 28, 2010, and available at
http://www.tulsaworld.com/sportsextra/OU/article.
aspx?subjectid=92&articleid=20080928_298_
Okla002744&archive=yes

"The Texas quarterback saw the Red River pairing as
special."
"Heisman Showdown," by John E. Hoover, *Tulsa World*,
October 10, 2008, and available at http://www.tulsaworld.
com/sportsextra/OU/article.aspx?subjectid=92&articleid=
20081010_92_B1_TomGil584717&archive=yes

"Sometimes," she said, her voice cracking, "you just have to
pinch yourself and realize what's happening."
"The Toast of New York," John E. Hoover, *Tulsa World*,
December 13, 2008, and available at http://www.tulsaworld.
com/sportsextra/OU/article.aspx?subjectid=92&articleid=2
0081213_92_B1_Heisma497939&archive=yes

"Earlier, the three of them had sat in the green room together . . ."
"It's Not Fair to Rip Tebow for His Faith," by Woody Paige, *The Denver Post*, May 4, 2010, and available at http://www.denverpost.com/paige/ci_15011076

"I first need to thank God . . ."
Transcription of Sam Bradford's Heisman Speech from this video: http://www.youtube.com/watch?v=VN-Nm-rRVC Y&feature=PlayList&p=89EC30B3EC5D9DB9&playnex t_from=PL&playnext=1&index=7

"Kent and Martha Bradford, whose memory banks must have flashed through the hundreds of peewee ballgames . . ."
"Sam's Club," by John E. Hoover, *Tulsa World*, December 14, 2008, and available at http://www.tulsaworld.com/sports-extra/OU/article.aspx?subjectid=92&articleid=20081214_9 2_B1_Olhmur737076&archive=yes

"Something else neat happened in New York: Sam clicked with Colt."
"QB Triumvirate Share Common Bond," by Ivan Maisel, ESPN.com, published August 12, 2009, and available at http://sports.espn.go.com/ncf/preview09/columns/ story?columnist=maisel_ivan&id=4391994

"The day after Sam cradled the Heisman Trophy, Jeremy Fowler of *The Orlando Sentinel* laid down a Gator gauntlet when he wrote . . ."
"Loss Will Only Fuel Tebow's Fire," by Jeremy Fowler, *The*

Orlando Sentinel, December 15, 2008, and available at
http://www.tulsaworld.com/sportsextra/OU/
article.aspx?subjectid=92&articleid=20081215_92_B2_
NEWYOR613627&archive=yes

"The trash talk began when Sooners cornerback Dominique
Franks . . ."
"Oklahoma DB Dominique Franks Says Tim Tebow Would
Be 4th-Best QB in Big 12," by Jeremy Fowler, *The Orlando
Sentinel*, January 5, 2009, and available at http://articles.
orlandosentinel.com/2009-01-05/sports/bcstebow05_1_
franks-oklahoma-defensive-oklahoma-sam-bradford

"Florida linebacker Brandon Spikes, however, couldn't
resist the microphone . . ."
"Tebow Responds: Gator Spikes Calls Big 12 Defenses 'A
Joke,' " by Guerin Emig and John E. Hoover, *Tulsa World*,
January 5, 2009, and available at http://www.tulsaworld.
com/sportsextra/OU/article.aspx?subjectid=92&articleid=2
0090105_92_0_MIAMIF579650&archive=yes

"You don't want to wake up a sleeping giant . . ."
"Florida's Tebow, Defense Power Past Oklahoma in BCS
Title," by B. G. Brooks, *Rocky Mountain News*, January 8,
2009, and available at http://www.rockymountainnews.com/
news/2009/jan/08/florida-tops-oklahoma-bcs-title-game/

"Kent also knew something about insurance policies . . ."
"Texas' Colt McCoy Joins Elite Quarterbacks Who Have
Insurance," Matt Murschel, *Orlando Sentinel*, July 26, 2009,

and available at http://blogs.orlandosentinel.com/sports_college/2009/07/texas-colt-mccoy-joins-elite-quarterbacks-who-have-insurance.html

"Kent declined to state how much insurance the family took out . . ."
"Good Thing Sam Bradford Has Insurance," The Sports Culture Web site, and available at http://thesportsculture.com/2009/09/07/good-thing-sam-bradford-has-insurance/

"One of the first questions asked was whether he had any regrets about deciding to return to the University of Oklahoma . . ."
"Bradford Says Farewell," Guerin Emig, *Tulsa World*, October 27, 2009, and available at http://www.tulsaworld.com/sportsextra/OU/article.aspx?subjectid=92&articleid=20091027_92_A1_SamBra540297&archive=yes

2. Colt McCoy: The Eyes of Texas Are upon Him

"Inside the Rose Bowl locker room . . ."
"Anguished McCoy Did All He Could to Change Ending," by Mike Lopresti, *USA Today*, January 8, 2010, and available at http://www.usatoday.com/sports/columnist/lopresti/2010-01-08-mccoy-anguish_N.htm

"It seemed like millions to Colt . . . ."
"Agonizing Night for Texas QBs," by Dan Wetzel, Yahoo Sports, January 8, 2010, and available at http://rivals.yahoo.com/ncaa/football/news?slug=dw-texasqbs010810

"During a lull in that game's action . . ."
"Title-Seeking QBs Share Football Pasts, Big Dreams of BCS
Glory," by Kelly Whiteside, *USA Today*, January 6, 2010,
and available at http://www.usatoday.com/sports/college/
football/2010-01-06-bcs-mccoy-mcelroy-cover_N.htm

"Keep your head up. Keep plugging away . . ."
"Garret Gilbert Bounces Back from BCS Title Game,"
by Chip Brown at Orangebloods.com, March 4,
2010, and available at http://texas.rivals.com/content.
asp?CID=1059086

"They also like to torture him by pretending to punch him
in the man region . . ."
"The Eyes of Texas Are upon Him," by Rick Reilly, ESPN.
com, published October 14, 2009, and available at
http://sports.espn.go.com/espn/columns/
story?columnist=reilly_rick&id=4557869&sportCat=ncf

"The story goes that Colt's mom, Debra . . ."
"Brad & Debra McCoy: Leaving a Legacy," by Mike Giles,
Dallas Christian Family magazine, and available at http://
dfwchristianfamily.com/cover/McCoy-Leaving-Legacy.php

"I can't remember," he said. "I was a little baby . . ."
"Christian Faith Fuels Heisman Front-Runner Colt McCoy,"
by Peter Elliot, EverydayChristian.com, October 9, 2009,
and available at http://www.everydaychristian.com/features/
story/5053/

"And be a leader . . ."
"Title-Seeking QBs Share Football Pasts, Big Dreams of BCS Glory," by Kelly Whiteside, *USA Today*, January 6, 2010, and available at http://www.usatoday.com/sports/college/football/2010-01-06-bcs-mccoy-mcelroy-cover_N.htm

"Only middle names, please . . . "
The information that Colt's brothers go by their middle names comes from an interview Colt did with ESPN's Dan Patrick on October 15, 2008. The link is: http://www.youtube.com/watch?v=pw5sYBa9VlM&feature=related

"They would prepare their children for the path, not the path for their children . . ."
"Brad McCoy: Four Principles for Raising Godly Children," a blog written by Amy of Everyday Bless, April 9, 2010, and available at http://walkman4.blogspot.com/2010/04/brad-mccoy-4-principlesraising-godly.html

"Brad says he raised Colt and his brothers in a disciplined home . . ."
"Brad & Debra McCoy: Leaving a Legacy," by Mike Giles, *Dallas Christian Family* magazine, and available at http://dfwchristianfamily.com/cover/McCoy-Leaving-Legacy.php

"His father signaled in the play for a screen pass . . ."
"Father Brad Adds to Colt Lore," by Danny Reagan, GoColtGo.com, October 18, 2006, and available at http://blogs.scripps.com/abil/colt/2006/10/father_brad_adds_to_colt_lore.html

"Athletes do not drink soda . . ."
"ESPN Covers Century Council: Olympic Athletes Take
Time to Teach Kids," by Alyssa Roenigk, *The Century
Council*, February 24, 2010, and available at http://www.
centurycouncil.org/content/espn-covers-century-council-
olympic-athletes-take-time-teach-kids

"We were at On the Border by Six Flags in Arlington . . ."
"The Real McCoy," by Jason King, Yahoo Sports, October
16, 2008, and available at http://rivals.yahoo.com/ncaa/
football/news?slug=jn-mccoy101708

"A guy told me after the third game Colt played as a
seventh grader . . ."
"The Heart of Texas," by Clay Meyer, *Sharing the Victory*
magazine, December 2009, and available at http://www.
sharingthevictory.com/vsItemDisplay.lsp?method=display&
objectid=3DE967BD-C29A-EE7A-E1312EF7698DA498

"I caught some criticism for it . . ."
"The Real McCoy," by Jason King, Yahoo Sports, October
16, 2008, and available at http://rivals.yahoo.com/ncaa/foot-
ball/news?slug=jn-mccoy101708

"Sign it," Lavallee replied. "It'll probably be the first of
many."
"The Real McCoy," by Jason King, Yahoo Sports, October
16, 2008, and available at http://rivals.yahoo.com/ncaa/
football/news?slug=jn-mccoy101708

"We got beat on a cold night . . ."
"Texas' Star-Studded Colt Not Playing Like a Freshman," by
Todd Henrichs, *Lincoln Journal Star*, October 19, 2006, and
available at http://journalstar.com/sports/football/college/
article_67340ae3-0675-52d7-a147-1d952b523e11.html

"I kind of did this [committing to the Longhorns] to get it
off my shoulders . . ."
Danny Reagan, *Abilene Reporter-News*, May 18, 2004, and
available at http://blogs.reporternews.com/colt/UTcommit-
ment.html

"At the start of training camp . . ."
"Title-Seeking QBs Share Football Pasts, Big Dreams of BCS
Glory," by Kelly Whiteside, *USA Today*, January 6, 2010,
and available at http://www.usatoday.com/sports/college/
football/2010-01-06-bcs-mccoy-mcelroy-cover_N.htm

" . . . Greg Davis remembers Colt approaching him the
day . . ."
"Colt McCoy of Texas Says He's the Best QB in NFL Draft,"
by Mary Kay Cabot, *Cleveland Plain Dealer*, April 17, 2010,
and available at http://www.cleveland.com/browns/index.
ssf/2010/04/cleveland_browns_prospect_colt.html

"I'm not listening to you, dude. You're a freshman . . ."
Q&A with QB Colt McCoy, posted on the 49ers.com Web
site April 12, 2010, and available at http://www.49ers.
com/news-and-events/article-2/QA-with-QB-Colt-
McCoy/508b5c93-73d0-483a-9d09-782f36328e6f

"I thought Vince would come back . . ."
"Mack's Media Day, Part One: The Quarterbacks," by
Peter Bean, Burnt Orange Nation Web site, July 25,
2006, and available at http://www.burntorangenation.
com/2006/7/25/142512/092

"You never enjoy losing, but losing to the Aggies is even
worse . . ."
"McGee Accounts for 4 TDs, Aggies beat No. 13 Texas
before A&M Coach Franchione Resigns," Associated Press,
November 24, 2007, and available at http://www.usatoday.
com/sports/scores107/107327/NCAAF763617.htm

"This is Patina. Ken and I are on the dock . . ."
Author's interview of Patina Herrington by the author,
April 16, 2010.

"It seems the translators had pooled their money . . ."
"Colt Hero," by Alyssa Roenig, *ESPN Magazine*, August 18,
2009, and available at http://sports.espn.go.com/ncf/news/
story?id=4395897

Reagan Lambert, who has been working with . . . "
Author's interview with Reagan Lambert, April 28, 2010.
"Nobody knows who you are. You can just be yourself for a
week . . ."
"Colt McCoy: Missionary Man," by Bill Frisbie, Inside Tex-
as.com, March 10, 2009, and available at http://insidetexas.
com/news/story.php?article=930

"It's not a slump because I feel like I grew so much . . ."
"Bradford, McCoy Debunk Predictions of Doom," by Dave
Sittler, *Tulsa World*, October 8, 2008, and available at
http://www.tulsaworld.com/sportsextra/article.as
px?subjectid=202&articleid=20081008_202_B1_
NORMAN313265&archive=yes

"McCoy escapes from seemingly impossible situations so
often . . ."
"Texas' McCoy Barely Beats Out OU's Bradford on My Final
Ballot," by Gene Menez, Sports Illustrated.com, December
8, 2008, and available at http://sportsillustrated.cnn.com/
2008/writers/gene_menez/12/08/final.heismanwatch/
#ixzz0llF4xifh

"Colt dedicated his 2008 season to the cousin . . ."
"McCoy Dedicating Season to Late Marine Cousin," by the
Associated Press, November 25, 2008, and available at
http://cbs11tv.com/sports/Colt.McCoy.Season.2.873700.
html

"It would mean a lot [to win against Alabama] . . . "
"2009 Sporting News College Athletes of the Year: Colt
McCoy, Texas QB," by Ken Bradley, The Sporting News,
December 17, 2009, and available at http://www.sporting-
news.com/college-football/article/2009-12-17/2009-sport-
ing-news-college-athlete-year-colt-mccoy-texas-qb

3. Tim Tebow: The Chosen One

"He's been called the NFL version's of a total solar eclipse . . ."
"Fame, Fortune and Being Tim Tebow," by Johnette
Howard, ESPN.com, April 22, 2010, and available at
http://sports.espn.go.com/espn/commentary/news/
story?page=howard/100422

"His agent, Jimmy Sexton, predicts Tim will become the
best marketable athlete in history . . ."
"Fame, Fortune and Being Tim Tebow," by Johnette
Howard, ESPN.com, April 22, 2010, and available at
http://sports.espn.go.com/espn/commentary/news/
story?page=howard/100422

"The Davie-Brown Index . . ."
"Not Even in NFL Yet, Tim Tebow Already a Marketing
Trendsetter," Associated Press, April 19, 2010, and available
at http://www.usatoday.com/sports/football/nfl/2010-04-19-
tim-tebow-marketing_N.htm?utm_source=moggy&utm_
medium=twitter&utm_campaign=GatorWire&utm_
source=GatorWire&utm_medium=twitter&utm_
campaign=MoggySocialMedia

"Growing up, I knew my goal was to get a job and make a
million dollars . . ."
"Tebow's Family Vision Runs Much Deeper Than Just TDs,"
by Dave Curtis, *South Florida Sun-Sentinel*, August 8, 2008,
and available at http://www.sun-sentinel.com/sports/other/
sfl-flsptebowdad08sbaug08,0,5446800.story

"Bob and Pam became friends, and their first date came a year after they met . . . "
"Coaching Character," by Suzy A. Richardson, *Gainesville Sun,* October 7, 2007, and available at http://www. gainesville.com/article/20071007/NEWS/710060317?p =all&tc=pgall

"It wasn't always easy, but it was a wonderful time for our family . . ."
"Coaching Character," by Suzy A. Richardson, *Gainesville Sun,* October 7, 2007, and available at http://www. gainesville. com/article/20071007/NEWS/710060317?p =all&tc=pgall

"I was weeping over the millions of babies being [aborted] in America . . ."
"You Gotta Love Tim Tebow," by Austin Murphy, *Sports Illustrated,* July 27, 2009, and available at http:// sportsillustrated.cnn.com/vault/article/magazine/ MAG1158168/index.htm

"Dysentery is common in developing and tropical countries like the Philippines . . ."
"Amoebic Dysentery: How Common Is It?" the British Medical Journal Group in association with the *Guardian* newspaper, March 9, 2010, and available at http://www.guardian.co.uk/lifeandstyle/besttreatments/ amoebic-dysentery-how-common

"They didn't really give me a choice. That was the only option they gave me . . ."
"Mothering Tebow," by Joni B. Hannigan, *Florida Baptist Witness*, January 8, 2009, and available at http://gofbw.com/News.asp?ID=9758

"It was amazing that God spared him, but we knew God had His hand on his life . . . "
"Mothering Tebow," by Joni B. Hannigan, *Florida Baptist Witness*, January 8, 2009, and available at http://gofbw.com/News.asp?ID=9758

"If I could get my kids to the age of 25 and they know God and serve God . . ."
"Tebows to Headline Evangelism Conference Sessions," *Florida Baptist Witness*, January 29, 2008, and available at http://www.gofbw.com/news.asp?ID=8334

"But the Tebows *were* into competition . . ."
"Competitive Fire Fuels Tebow," by Guerry Smith, Rivals.com Web site, December 8, 2007, and available at http://collegefootball.rivals.com/content.asp?cid=748732

"Some of his teammates were picking at the ground without even paying attention . . ."
"Competitive Fire Fuels Tebow," by Guerry Smith, Rivals.com Web site, December 8, 2007, and available at http://collegefootball.rivals.com/content.asp?cid=748732

"One time, Tim wrote a report on why athletes' bodies need more protein . . ."

"Pam Tebow's Labor of Love," by Lindsay H. Jones, *Denver Post*, May 10, 2010, and available at http://www.gainesville.com/article/20100510/ARTICLES/100519941?p=all&tc=pgall&tc=ar

"Guess that's my claim to fame . . ."
"Tebow Caused a Stir Even as a Youngster," by Dave Curtis, *Orlando Sentinel*, December 5, 2007, and available at http://articles.orlandosentinel.com/2007-12-05/sports/tebowthekid05_1_quarterback-tim-tebow-hess-allen

"That's not what Bob Tebow wanted for his son, though . . ."
"Team Tebow," by Robbie Andreu, *Gainesville Sun*, January 31, 2006, and available at http://www.gainesville.com/article/20060131/GATORS01/201310351?p=all&tc=pgall&tc=ar

"We wanted to give Tim the opportunity to develop his God-given talent . . ."
"Parents, High School Officials at Odds Over Motivation for Athletes' Transfers," by Ray Glier, *USA Today*, November 21, 2006, and available at http://www.usatoday.com/sports/preps/2006-11-21-transfers-cover_x.htm

"We were willing to make that sacrifice. We have made sacrifices for all our children . . ."
"QB Facing College Challenges Grounded in Christ," by Barbara Denman, *Florida Baptist Witness*, January 17, 2006, and available at http://www.gofbw.com/news.asp?ID=5351

"People can always lead with words but not always with actions . . ."
"A Gator for God," by Suzy Richardson, *Charisma*, October 2008, and available at http://www.charismamag.com/index.php/features/2008/october/17874-a-gator-for-god

"We had six road games my sophomore year . . ."
"Tim Tebow Draws from High School Days at Nease," by Mitch Stephens at MaxPreps.com, February 16, 2010, and available at http://www.maxpreps.com/news/Am-VWLhtREd-UswAcxJTdpg/tim-tebow-draws-from-high-school-days-at-nease.htm

"Chris Leak is our quarterback . . . "
"Orange Defeats Blue in a Less Than Spectacular Spring Finale," by Dennis Culver, *Gainesville Sun*, April 26, 2006, and available at http://www.gainesville.com/article/20060422/GATORS0108/60422003?p=all&tc=pgall

"There's room for another one next year, Timmy Tebow . . ."
"Leak, Wuerffel Share Lifetime Gator Bond," by Pat Dooley, *Gainesville Sun*, January 14, 2007, and available at http://www.gainesville.com/article/20070114/GATORS24/70114040?p=all&tc=pgall&tc=ar

"The story noted that Tim had sung 'She Thinks My Tractor's Sexy' . . . "
"A Florida Folk Hero Prepares to Face Reality," by Pete Thamel, *New York Times*, September 1, 2007, and available at http://www.nytimes.com/2007/09/01/sports/ncaafootball/01florida.html?_r=1

"After the Tennessee game, the *Gainesville Sun* collected the best quotes . . ."
"UF's Tebow a Legend of the Fall," *Gainesville Sun*, September 20, 2007, and available at http://www.gainesville. com/article/20070920/NEWS/709200331

"It makes you realize that everything that happens in this game doesn't really mean that much in the grand scheme of things . . ."
"Notebook: UF's Tebow Takes Losses Hard, Gains Perspective," by Brandon Zimmerman, *Gainesville Sun*, October 30, 2007, and available at http://www.gainesville.com/article/20071030/NEWS/710300310?tc=ar

"Tim took some hits from the media . . ."
"John 3:16—Latest Bible Verse to Be Featured on Tim Tebow's Eye Black," by Tom Herrera, *NCAA Football Fanhouse*, January 9, 2009, and available at http://ncaafootball.fanhouse.com/2009/01/09/john-3-16-latest-bible-verse-to-be-featured-on-tim-tebow/

"He's just an amazing young man, an amazing football player . . ."
"Tebow Wins Wuerffel Award," by Robbie Andreu, *Gainesville Sun*, December 9, 2008, and available at http://www.gainesville.com/article/20081209/NEWS/812090943

"You knew he was going to lead us to victory . . ."
"Tebow Engineers Comeback," by Kevin Brockway,

Gainesville Sun, December 7, 2008, and available at
http://www.gainesville.com/article/20081207/
NEWS/812060925

"I was pretty excited . . . "
"Best Player Ever? I'll Take Tebow" by Pat Dooley,
Gainesville Sun, January 9, 2009, and available at
http://www.gainesville.com/article/20090109/COLUMNIST
S/901090279?p=all&tc=pgall&tc=ar

4. Plenty of Predraft Drama

"I look at myself as a pretty self-motivated person . . ."
"Tebow Will 'Just Be Me' at Senior Bowl," Associated Press,
January 24, 2010, and available at http://www.gainesville.com
/article/20100124/ARTICLES/100129731?p=all&tc=pgall

" 'It's simple,' said one NFL scout . . ."
"Tim Tebow Senior Bowl: Disaster or First Step to NFL?"
by Mark Sappenfield, *Christian Science Monitor*, January
31, 2010, and available at http://www.csmonitor.com/USA/
Society/2010/0131/Tim-Tebow-Senior-Bowl-Disaster-or-
first-step-to-NFL

"Scouts Inc. gave Tim a D+ grade . . ."
"2010 Senior Bowl: Tim Tebow's Performance Adds to His
Plummeting NFL Draft Stock," by Daniel Wolf, Bleacher
Report.com, January 30, 2010, and available at
http://bleacherreport.com/articles/336387-tim-tebow-senior-
bowl-performance-adds-to-plummeting-nfl-draft-stock

"No mention of abortion . . ."
"Tim Tebow's Brilliant Fake Leads to Pro-Life Score," by
David Gibson, PoliticsDaily.com, February 7, 2007, and
available at http://www.politicsdaily.com/2010/02/07/
tim-tebows-brilliant-fake-leads-to-pro-life-score/

"At a speech held at Lipscomb University in Nashville . . ."
"Tebow Laughs Off Jerry Jones Video, Talks About Losing
Sponsors Because of His Super Bowl Ad," by Ben Volin,
Palm Beach Post, April 18, 2010, and available at
http://blogs.palmbeachpost.com/gatorbytes/2010/04/18/
tebow-laughs-off-jerry-jones-video-incident/

"It's more of a tweak . . ."
"Tim Tebow's New Team Honing His Technique," by Sam
Farmer, *Los Angeles Times*, February 27, 2010, and available
at http://articles.latimes.com/2010/feb/27/sports/la-sp-nfl-
combine27-2010feb27

"Kurt Hester, the corporate director of training at D1 . . ."
"What's It Like to Help Tim Tebow Prepare for the NFL?
D1's Kurt Hester Is Here to Tell You," by Ben Volin, *Palm
Beach Post*, February 22, 2010, and available at
http://blogs.palmbeachpost.com/gatorbytes/2010/02/22/
whats-it-like-to-help-tim-tebow-prepare-for-the-nfl-d1s-
kurt-hester-is-here-to-tell-you/

"You're investing a lot of money in some of these guys . . ."
"Future Pros Tackle Grueling NFL Combine," by Kevin
Acee, *San Diego Union-Tribune*, February 28, 2010, and

available at http://www.signonsandiego.com/news/2010/
feb/28/future-football-pros-tackle-grueling-days-combine/

"You get dizzy from it all . . ."
"Underwear Olympics," by Phil King, *Sports Illustrated*, pg.
61, March 8, 2010.

"I'd like to say I was six-foot-four . . ."
"Colt McCoy Doesn't Shy Away from Brees Comparison,"
by Jason Feller, NFL.com, February 27, 2010, and available
at http://blogs.nfl.com/2010/02/27/colt-mccoy-doesnt-shy-
away-from-brees-comparison/

"Here are some sample questions from the Wonderlic
test . . ."
"So How Do You Score?" ESPN page 2, and available at
http://espn.go.com/page2/s/closer/020228test.html

"For all the television time, Internet bandwidth . . ."
"Florida's Pro Day Was a True Circus, with Tim Tebow
Front and Center," by Andy Staples, SI.com, March 18, 2010,
and available at http://sportsillustrated.cnn.com/2010/writ-
ers/andy_staples/03/17/tim.tebow.pro.day/index.html

"The 15 minutes passed by way too quickly . . ."
"Tebow Quickly Impressed McDaniels, Broncos as a
Genuine Gem," by Lindsay H. Jones, *The Denver Post*, April
25, 2010, and available at http://www.denverpost.com/
broncos/ci_14953999

"I like this workout better . . ."
"McCoy Satisfied He Aces Test at Texas Pro Day," by
Charean Williams, The Sports XChange/CBSSports.com,
and available at http://www.cbssports.com/nfl/draft/story/
13141671/mccoy-satisfied-he-aces-test-at-texas-pro-day

"Colt said he enjoyed his 'pitch and catch' . . ."
"McCoy Accurate in Workout," by the Associated Press,
April 1, 2010, and available at http://sports.espn.go.com/nfl/
draft10/news/story?id=5044786

5. The 2010 NFL Draft

"When quarterbacks Peyton Manning and Ryan Leaf were
in the running . . ."
"Leaf's Pro Career: Short and Unhappy," by Damon Hack,
New York Times, August 4, 2002, and available at
http://www.nytimes.com/2002/08/04/sports/pro-football-
leaf-s-pro-career-short-and-unhappy.html

"Everything you hear about him, that's said, it's legit . . ."
"Rams Keeping a Close Eye on Bradford as Prospective No.
1," by Jim Thomas, *St. Louis Post-Dispatch*, April 21, 2010,
and available at http://www.stltoday.com/stltoday/sports/
stories.nsf/rams/story/604C46ED60B319BB862576F10005F
645?OpenDocument

" . . . Devaney learned a valuable lesson when it came to
drafting quarterbacks . . ."
"Evaluating Quarterbacks Is a Tough Part of the Draft," by

Jim Thomas, *St. Louis Post-Dispatch*, April 12, 2010, and
available at http://www.stltoday.com/stltoday/sports/stories.
nsf/rams/story/EB21CD1FB9FB34B686257703000EA4B3?
OpenDocument

"It's a once-in-a-lifetime thing . . ."
"Bradford Discusses Decision to Attend NFL Draft," by John
E. Hoover, *Tulsa World*, April 22, 2010, and available at
http://www.tulsaworld.com/sportsextra/OU/
article.aspx?subjectid=92&articleid=20100422_92_0
_NEWYOR504083&archive=yes

"In a conference call with St. Louis reporters . . . "
"St. Louis Rams Get Their Man in QB Sam Bradford," by
Jim Thomas, *St. Louis Post-Dispatch*, April 23, 2010, and
available at http://www.stltoday.com/stltoday/sports/stories.
nsf/rams/story/25E7CB0AEC82E9348625770E00146973?O
penDocument

"It would have been exciting to be here . . ."
"Tebow Declines Invitations to Attend Draft, Decides
to Return Home," by Jason La Canfora, NFL.com, April
21, 2010, and available at http://www.nfl.com/draft/sto
ry?id=09000d5d817aa5ce&template=with-video-with-
comments&confirm=true

"Tim's former teammate at Florida, Cincinnati Bengals wide
receiver Andre Caldwell . . ."
"Bengals' Andre Caldwell: Right Spot to Pick Tim Tebow Is
'Late Second Round,' *USA Today*'s The Huddle, March 31,

2010, and available at http://content.usatoday.com/com-
munities/thehuddle/post/2010/03/bengals-andre-caldwell-
right-spot-to-pick-tim-tebow-is-late-second-round/1

"Miami Dolphins quarterback Chad Henne . . ."
"Dolphins' Chad Henne on Tim Tebow: 'He's Not an NFL
Quarterback,'" *USA Today*'s The Huddle, March 18, 2010,
and available at http://content.usatoday.com/communities/
thehuddle/post/2010/03/dolphins-chad-henne-hes-not-an-
nfl-quarterback/1

" . . . Tim did an interview on ESPN Radio with host
Freddie Coleman . . ."
"Time Tebow Does Not Take Mel Kiper's Criticism Kindly,
Calls Him Out on Air," by Will Brinson, NCAA Football
Fanhouse, December 19, 2008, and available at
http://ncaafootball.fanhouse.com/2008/12/19/tim-tebow-
does-not-take-mel-kipers-criticism-kindly-calls-him/

"On the morning of the NFL draft . . . "
"Tim Tebow: Is He a Miracle Worker, or Just an Average
QB?" by Jon Saraceno, *USA Today*, April 22, 2010, and
available at http://www.usatoday.com/sports/football/
nfl/2010-04-21-tim-tebow_N.htm

"If you want Tim to be on your football team . . ."
"Great Tebow Draft Debate Will Finally Be Answered," by
Robbie Andreu, *Gainesville Sun*, April 21, 2010, and
available at http://www.gainesville.com/article/20100421/
ARTICLES/100429878?p=all&tc=pgall&tc=ar

"Whether it's Tim Tebow . . . you look for a guy with good
character . . ."
"Report: Tebow Plans Team Workouts," by ESPN.com,
March 8, 2010, and available at http://sports.espn.go.com/
nfl/draft10/news/story?id=4974087

"Kiper and his ESPN sidekick, Todd McShay, stuck to their
guns . . ."
"Great Tebow Draft Debate Will Finally Be Answered," by
Robbie Andreu, *Gainesville Sun*, April 21, 2010, and
available at http://www.gainesville.com/article/20100421/A
RTICLES/100429878?p=all&tc=pgall&tc=ar

"Klis then offered these reasons . . ."
"Will the Broncos Draft Tim Tebow?" by Mike Klis, *The
Denver Post,* April 21, 2010, and available at http://blogs.
denverpost.com/broncos/2010/04/21/the-case-for-tebow/

"And that's when Tim's cell phone rang with a 303 area
code . . ."
"Tim Tebow Drafted by Denver Broncos in First Round of
NFL Draft," by Jeremy Fowler, *South Florida Sun-Sentinel,*
April 23, 2010, and available at http://articles.sun-sentinel.
com/2010-04-23/sports/sfl-tim-tebow-broncos-10_1_
tim-tebow-25th-selection-later-round

"Coach McDaniels was on the line, but he didn't seem at all
in a hurry . . ."
"Mile-High on Tebow," by Robbie Andreu, *Gainesville Sun*,
April 23, 2010, and available at http://www.gainesville.com/

article/20100423/ARTICLES/4231012?p=all&tc=pgall&tc=ar

"I just think I showed them [the Broncos] I was willing to do whatever it took . . ."
"Tim Tebow Drafted by the Denver Broncos," Alligator Army Web site, April 22, 2010, and available at http://www.alligatorarmy.com/2010/4/22/1437123/tim-tebow-drafted-by-the-denver

"Tim Tebow is a lightning rod . . ."
"Colorado Evangelicals Singing Praises of McDaniels' QB Pick Tebow," by Electa Draper, *The Denver Post*, April 24, 2010, and available at http://www.denverpost.com/news/ci_14948943

"A couple of NFL scouts, speaking anonymously, told CBS Sports . . ."
"Clausen's Fall to Second Round and Panthers Gets Personal," by Clark Judge, CBSSports.com, May 6, 2010, and available at http://www.cbssports.com/nfl/story/13355576/clausens-fall-to-second-round-and-panthers-gets-personal

"Devaney said afterward that Colt was extremely impressive . . ."
"Rams Impressed with Colt McCoy During Private Workout," by Laken Litman, SportsDayDFW by *The Dallas Morning News*, April 9, 2010, and available at http://collegesportsblog.dallasnews.com/archives/2010/04/rams-impressed-with-colt-mccoy-during-pr.html

"Don't worry, Son, you're in a great place . . ."
"Browns' Mike Holmgren Takes an Ordinary Joe in Colt McCoy," by Rick Gosselin, SportsDayDFW by *The Dallas Morning News*, April 24, 2010, and available at http://www.dallasnews.com/sharedcontent/dws/spt/columnists/rgosselin/stories/042410dnspogosselincolumn.410e13f.html

"Nobody expected Colt to have the career that he had at Texas . . ."
"Browns' Mike Holmgren Takes an Ordinary Joe in Colt McCoy," by Rick Gosselin, SportsDayDFW by *The Dallas Morning News*, April 24, 2010, and available at http://www.dallasnews.com/sharedcontent/dws/spt/columnists/rgosselin/stories/042410dnspogosselincolumn.410e13f.html

"Tim bowed his head and delivered a wonderful prayer . . ."
"Tim Tebow Closes National Prayer Breakfast in Prayer, But Obama Leaves," by Steven Ertelt, LifeNews.com, February 4, 2010, and available at http://www.lifenews.com/nat5964.html